IRENE BOTSFORD HOFFMANN

THE BOOK
OF
Herb Cookery

REVISED EDITION

GRAMERCY PUBLISHING COMPANY · NEW YORK

ACKNOWLEDGMENTS

ACKNOWLEDGMENT and thanks are made to the Massachusetts Horticultural Society for permission to use certain notes from the book, *Herbs: How to Grow Them and How to Use Them*, written for that Society by Helen Noyes Webster, to whom I am also greatly indebted for much help in preparing this volume.

I want also to express my thanks to Lucy Roviaro for her intelligent and interested co-operation in this adventure in Herb Cookery.

And to my family, whose patience and encouragement during a long period of trial and error have been unfailing.

I. B. H.

DEDICATED
TO
THE MEMBERS OF THE

BERKSHIRE GARDEN CENTER

IN RESPONSE TO THEIR INTEREST
IN THE HERB GARDEN AND DESIRE
TO LEARN THE PRACTICAL USES OF
THE PLANTS GROWN THERE

CONTENTS

INTRODUCTION

ON THE USE OF HERBS IN COOKERY

THE question may well be asked — why another cookbook? Are there not already enough books written on the art of cooking everything — in every way — by every famous person — to give us permanent mental if not physical indigestion!

And herbs, too, have received so much attention of late that there is no longer any excuse for the question, What do you do with them? Haven't we been told by experts how to know them; how to grow them (or where to buy them); how to eat them, drink them, dry them, smell them, arrange them in tussie-mussies; and how to use them to keep away mice and moths, ants and flies! But most of these excellent books on herbs cover such a wide field of their many and varied uses that cookery plays a minor rôle; directions are sometimes casual or vague and recipes few. This book, then, treats only of the culinary herbs and is an attempt to list and classify, in orderly cookbook fashion, a number of recipes for preparing a variety of foods the flavor of which is enhanced or improved by the addition of herbs. Flavoring is an art and should be subtle and illusive. It is very easy to use too much — the 'heavy hand' must be restrained.

The word *herb*, which is usually defined as 'a fragrant plant with medicinal or culinary use,' is here given the broader interpretation of the herbalists of former days, who did not distinguish between *herbs* and vegetables in general.

The book will therefore include a chapter on vegetables and vegetable entrées; and as no well-balanced meal is complete without fruit, one section is devoted to the serving of fresh and cooked fruit with recipes for fruit desserts.

In cooking with herbs the fresh ones are naturally to be preferred when obtainable, but for those who have no garden, the market supply is usually limited to parsley, chives, and mint. It is now possible to obtain a greater variety of dried herbs; one should be certain that they are reasonably fresh and have not been in stock a year or more. Dried herbs should be used much more sparingly than the fresh ones: one teaspoon dried herbs to one tablespoon fresh is a good rule to follow. Many recipes, notably French ones, are necessarily vague as to directions and quantities — the French, being born cooks, can be trusted to know by instinct what is meant by 'a little bit of this or a little bit of that,' or 'a good handful'; but most of us require more specific directions. In using herbs for the first time, experiment with caution; but combine them with imagination and common sense and you will have rewarding results and cooking will become a new adventure.

No excuse is needed for stressing the greater use of herbs in cooking. It is not a fad, it is nothing new. The best cooks of all European countries have never ceased to use them as a matter of course. It is we in America who have forgotten our heritage of the art of flavoring and seasoning, of the art of wholesome and delicious cooking brought to this country by our ancestors.

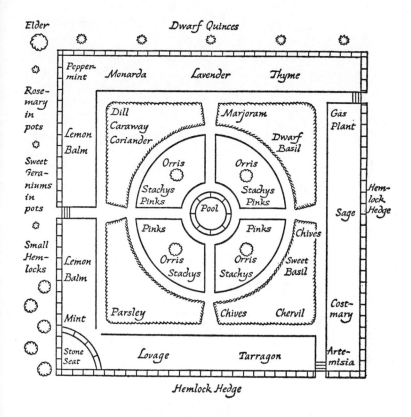

Plan for a Sunken Herb Garden

20' by 20'

Paving stones edged with Dwarf Thyme
Corner beds edged with clipped Artemisia

CHAPTER I

ALPHABETICAL LIST OF CULINARY HERBS

The following list of about fifty herbs includes all those ordinarily used in cookery. It might be extended to include more of the rare and unusual varieties, but many of the latter are difficult to obtain, or so little known or used that it might merely confuse the average cook and perhaps discourage her in the very beginning of her adventure in herb cookery

ANGELICA ARCHANGELICA OFFICINALIS *or* ANGELICA ARCHANGELICA

Parts used: leaves or stalks

An ingredient in liqueurs, Chartreuse and Bénédictine.
A liqueur (p. 176)

Candied stalks (p. 219)
Jam
To flavor rhubarb (p. 211)

ANISE PIMPINELLA ANISUM

Parts used: seeds and leaves

SEEDS in cookies and cakes (p. 238)

Applesauce

Beet salad

LEAVES

Sometimes chopped over carrots and in salads
Tisane (p. 168)

Confections
Liqueur anisette

BALM MELISSA OFFICINALIS (LEMON BALM)

Parts used: leaves

For wine (p. 176)
Flavoring drinks

Tea (p. 168)
Fruit punch (p. 171)

BASIL OCIMUM BASILICUM O. MINIMUM O. CRISPUM ('lettuce-leaved')

Parts used: leaves

All these are much used in
Italy to flavor tomato dishes
In soups (pp. 30, 31)
In sauces (pp. 84, 85)
For seasoning sausages (p. 61)
and calves' liver
In Court Bouillon for fish
(p. 33)

Tomato cocktails (p. 174)
In salads (p. 150)
In fine herbs (p. 12)
Maître d'hôtel sauce
Basil vinegar (p. 225)

BAY LAURUS NOBILIS (SWEET BAY)

Parts used: leaves

For flavoring soups, sauces,
stews, etc. (p. 14)

In combination with other herbs
for bouquet garni (p. 12)

BORAGE BORAGO OFFICINALIS

Parts used: flowers and leaves

FLOWERS
Candied and used for decora-
tion (p. 219)
LEAVES
Have a flavor of cucumber and

are used for: claret cup, cider
cup, and for various fruit
punches (p. 171). Tips may
also be used in salad.

BURNET SANGUISORBA OFFICINALIS
S. OFF. VAR. MINOR — SALAD BURNET

Parts used: leaves

While both burnets are good
for flavoring, S. minor is
more desirable and delicate.
The salad burnet is, as its

name implies, used in salads — with cucumbers es-
pecially — and to flavor vinegar.

CAMOMILE MATRICARIA CAMOMILLA (GERMAN CAMOMILE)

Parts used: blossoms

For tea (medicinal) (p. 168)

CARAWAY   CARUM CARVI

Parts used: seeds

In rye bread
In seed cakes (p. 236)
In seed cookies (p. 238)
To flavor cheese (p. 162)
With cabbage

With beets
Goulash (p. 50)
Liqueur 'Kümmel'
Candies

CARDAMOM   ELETTARIA CARDAMOM

Parts used: seeds

In cookies (p. 237)
In pastry
In breads, 'Swedish Boller'
(p. 235)
Honigkuchen (p. 231)

Gingerbread (p. 236)
An ingredient of curry pow-
der (p. 77)
An ingredient in liqueurs

CELERY   APIUM SATIVUM

Parts used: seeds, leaves, and stalks

For flavoring soups, stews, etc.

As a vegetable (pp. 126, 127)

CHERVIL   ANTHRISCUS CEREFOLIUM

Parts used: leaves and sometimes fleshy root

In place of parsley
In fine herbs (p. 12), salads,
sauces (p. 76), soups (p. 17)

In omelets, cheese, etc. (pp. 88,
163

CHIVES   ALLIUM SCHOENOPRASUM

Parts used: leaves

Indispensable as an ingredient
of fine herbs (p. 12)
For salads (p. 150), omelets

(p. 88), or anything for
which a delicate onion flavor
is desired

CORIANDER   CORIANDRUM SATIVUM

Parts used: seeds

An ingredient in curry powder
(p. 77)
To flavor cookies, honey cakes,
candies, and gingerbread

Cordials, gin

COSTMARY CHRYSANTHEMUM BALSAMITA
VAR. TANACETOIDES ('BIBLE LEAF')

Parts used: leaves

For negus To flavor roast beef
To flavor Hamburg steaks

CRESSES

GARDEN *or* PEPPER CRESS (LEPIDIUM SATIVUM)

Parts used: leaves

Good in salads (pp. 150, 155) and sandwiches (p. 164)

UPLAND CRESS, GARDEN FORM (BARBAREA PRAECOX)

Salads (p. 156)

WATER CRESS (RADICULA NASTURTIUM AQUATICUM)

Salads (pp. 152, 153, 157) Sandwiches (p. 164)
Soups (pp. 18, 32)

CUMIN CUMINUM CYMINUM

Parts used: seeds

An ingredient in curry powder Sugar cookies
(p. 77)

DANDELION TARAXACUM OFFICINALS

Parts used: leaves and buds

LEAVES FLOWER HEADS
For greens (p. 132) For wine (p. 174)
In salads (p. 156)

DILL ANETHUM GRAVEOLENS

Parts used: seeds and young tips

SEEDS In potato salad (p. 155)
In dill pickles (p. 128) Sprinkled on broiled chops
YOUNG TIPS (p. 51)
Cut up with cucumbers (p. 160) With cheese (p. 163)
For fish sauces (p. 77)

FENNEL FOENICULUM OFFICINALS

Parts used: seeds and leaves

For fish (pp. 33, 34, 40) In soup (p. 18)
In sauces (pp. 40, 78) In omelet (p. 88)

FINOCCHIO   FOENICULUM DULCE, SWEET FENNEL — FLORENCE FENNEL

Parts used: fleshy leaf bases

Eaten raw like celery, excellent
with Bel Paese cheese
In salad (p. 154)

Braised (p. 131)
Au gratin (p. 131)

FLAGROOT   ACORUS CALAMUS

Part used: root

Candied (p. 220)

GARLIC   ALLIUM SATIVUM

Parts used: 'cloves' (division of compound bulb)

To flavor salads (p. 149)
To flavor meats (p. 45)

To flavor soups
To flavor sauces (p. 78)

GERANIUMS   PELARGONIUM GRAVEOLENS, TOMENTOSUM, ETC.

Parts used: leaves

The leaves of the sweet-
scented varieties, such as

rose, peppermint, or *lemon,*
to flavor jellies (p. 222)

GOOD KING HENRY   CHENOPODIUM BONUS HENRICUS

Parts used: leaves and midribs

YOUNG LEAVES
For greens (p. 132)

MIDRIBS
Cooked in cream

HOREHOUND   MARRUBIUM VULGARE

Parts used: leaves, stems, and flowers

In candy (pp. 220, 221)

HORSERADISH   COCHLEARIA ARMORACIA

Part used: root

Sauces (p. 79)

LEEKS   ALLIUM PORRUM

Parts used: blanched leaf portions

Soups (p. 20)
Salads (p. 155)

As a vegetable (p. 134)

LEMON VERBENA   LIPPIA CITRIODORA

Parts used: leaves

For tisanes   For flavoring cold drinks

LOVAGE   LEVISTICUM OFFICINALE

Parts used: leaves, stem, root

LEAVES AND STEM
Strong celery flavor, used to
flavor soups or stews
Tomato cocktail (p. 174)

ROOT
Formerly candied like flagroot
(p. 220)

MARIGOLD   CALENDULA OFFICINALIS

Parts used: florets

Formerly used in puddings and
custards (p. 194)

In pudding sauces (p. 194)
Cordial (p. 177)

MARJORAM (SWEET)   ORIGANUM MARJORANA

Parts used: leaves

Sprinkled over beef, lamb, or
pork
Used in veal stew (p. 56)
Used in chopped meat
Used in meatballs

Cooked with zucchini (p. 143)
An ingredient in fine herbs
(p. 12)
In salads (p. 157)

MARJORAM (POT)   ORIGANUM ONITES

Parts used: leaves
Used for soups or stews

MINTS   MENTHA

APPLE   (M. ROTUNDIFOLIA)

APPLE VARIEGATED GOLDEN   (M. GENTILIS)

CURLY   (M. SPICATA VAR. CRISPA)

ORANGE   (M. PIPERITA VAR. CITRATA)

PEPPERMINT   (M. PIPERITA)

SPEARMINT   (M. SPICATA)

Parts used: leaves

To flavor sauces (p. 80),
vegetables (p. 123), in jellies (p. 222) fruit drinks

(pp. 169–174), tea (p. 169),
julep (p. 172), candy (p. 220)

MUSTARD   BRASSICA ALBA (WHITE)

Parts used: young leaves

For salads (p. 133)
For greens (p. 133)
In sandwiches (p. 164)

MUSTARD   B. NIGRA (BLACK)

Parts used: seeds

In pickles (p. 128)
For cooking, etc., and ground for the mustard of commerce

NASTURTIUM   TROPAEOLEUM MAJUS

Parts used: leaves, flowers, and seeds

LEAVES AND FLOWERS
In salad (p. 156)

SEEDS
Pickled, used as capers

ONION   ALLIUM CEPA

Part used: bulb

To flavor soups, meats, sauces, salads, entrées, and other vegetables
As a vegetable (p. 136)

PARSLEY   PETROSELINUM HORTENSE

Parts used: leaves

In fine herbs (p. 12)
In bouquet garni (p. 12)
For soups (p. 25)
For sauces (p. 30)
Greens
Tisane

Other varieties
Curly or mossleaf
Plain or Italian
    Uses are the same as above.
Parsnip-rooted or Hamburg.
    Plain leaves. Roots may be boiled and used in salads, soups, etc.

PURSLANE   PORTULACA OLERACEA

Part used: plant

Cooked for greens (p. 133)
Soup bonne femme (p. 28)

Young leaves, for salad

RAMPION   CAMPANULA RAPUNCULOIDES

Part used: root

Formerly cooked and served as salad or vegetable

ROSEMARY   ROSEMARINUS OFFICINALIS

Parts used: leaves

To flavor roast lamb **(p. 54)**
    and veal (p. 58)
Meat stews (p. 53)

Herb soup (p. **29**)
Tisane (p. 169)

RUE   RUTA GRAVEOLENS

Parts used: leaves

With cheese
In sandwiches

In salads
In vegetable cocktails

SAFFLOWER   CARTHAMUS TINCTORIUS (FALSE SAFFRON)

Parts used: florets

Much used in place of the true saffron

SAFFRON   CROCUS SATIVUS (TRUE SAFFRON)

Parts used: stigmas of flower

To flavor and color rice dishes
    (pp. 103, 105)

For bouillabaisse (p. 35) **and**
    other fish dishes

SAGE   SALVIA OFFICINALIS

Parts used: leaves

Stuffing (p. 61)
Cheese (p. 162)
Tea (p. 169)

Sage and onion sauce for roast
    pork (p. 81)
Fish chowder (p. 36)

SUMMER SAVORY   SATUREIA HORTENSIS

Parts used: leaves

Cooked with beans (p. 119)
One of the ingredients of fine

herbs (p. **12**)
With split pea soup (p. 28)

WINTER SAVORY   SATUREIA MONTANA

Parts used: leaves

To flavor meats and meat
    sauces
Has a different flavor and is

stronger and more peppery
than summer savory

SESAME   SESAMUM INDICUM
Parts used: seeds
For cookies (p. 237), cakes, or rolls

Candy

SHALLOT   ALLIUM ASCALONICUM
Parts used: compound bulb parts called cloves
Of milder flavor than onion and used in the same ways

The leaves may be used like chives

SKIRRET   SIUM SISARUM
Part used: root
Boiled as vegetable or salad

SORREL   RUMEX SCUTATUS
Parts used: leaves
For soups (pp. 19, 29)
Purée (p. 140)

With spinach (p. 142)
With egg dishes (p. 88)

TARRAGON   ARTEMISIA DRACUNCULUS
Parts used: leaves
In sauces (pp. 75, 78, 82)
In salads (pp. 150, 153)
To flavor chicken (pp. 68, 69) and other meats (pp. 48, 50, 57)

For egg and tomato dishes
Sandwiches
In fine herbs (p. 12)
Liqueur (p. 177)
Vinegar (p. 225)

THYMES   THYMUS VULGARIS (ENGLISH THYME, 'BROAD-LEAVED')
Parts used: leaves
In herb bouquets and fine herbs (p. 12)

In stews, soups, sauces

FRENCH THYME ('*narrow-leaved*') is used like the English
LEMON-SCENTED THYME   T. SERPYLLUM VAR. CITRIODORUS
Parts used: leaves
To flavor tea or cold drinks, or anything in which a mild lemon flavor is desired.
There are many more varieties of thyme; too many to list. These are more commonly

used in wall and rock plantings or between paving stones, but almost all of them may have culinary uses.

WOODRUFF ASPERULA ODORATA

Parts used: leaves and flowers, fresh or dried

An ingredient of the famous German punch, 'Mai Bowle,' May Bowl (p. 170) made always in the spring when the tiny white flowers appear.

Known as 'Waldmeister,' it is also used in its dried state, but the fresh herb is much to be preferred.

WORMWOOD ARTEMISIA ABSINTHIUM

Parts used: leaves

To flavor wine (absinthe, vermouth)
Tea (medicinal) (p. 169)

In cocktail (absinthe) (p. 173)
In coolers (vermouth) (p. 173)

CHAPTER II

SOUPS

LIST OF RECIPES

The HERB BOUQUET is in such frequent demand, for soups, for stews, in the cooking of vegetables, that it is important to understand just what is meant by the term. It is a bunch of three or four fresh herbs tied together, which is removed after cooking. It may be varied, but the classic combination, unless otherwise specified, consists of parsley, celery leaves, an onion, and a sprig of thyme.

Some good combinations for special purposes are as follows:

Ravigote
(good with beef) { Burnet
Chervil
Chives
Tarragon

For Lamb Stew { Parsley
Thyme   or
Clove } { Rosemary
Parsley
Celery }

For Veal Stew { Sweet Marjoram
Parsley
Onion }

For Pea Soups { Rosemary
Celery   or
Parsley } { Thyme
Celery   or
Parsley } { Mint
Parsley }

For Tomato Soup { Basil
Parsley
Onion
Bay leaf }

FINE HERBS (*fines herbes*): a mixture, finely minced, of four or five herbs in different combinations, but always including chives and either parsley or chervil.

Chives, parsley, burnet, tarragon, chervil (Ravigote).

Chives, chervil, basil, burnet, thyme.

Chives, burnet, tarragon, marjoram, parsley.

Chives, chervil, savory, burnet.

Tarragon, although an ingredient of Ravigote and other fine-herb combinations, has such a distinctive and individual flavor that it is really better used alone, or at any rate not with other herbs of strong flavor such as thyme, summer savory, basil, or rosemary. Nor should thyme and summer savory be used together, as they are both of strong individual flavors. The beginner should err on the side of too little rather than too much. It is as easy to over-flavor as to over-season, and one flavor should never be allowed to kill another. Tarragon should never be allowed to cook more than a few minutes in soups or sauces; it should be added at the last.

Cut fine herbs with a small pair of scissors kept solely for that purpose.

If the dried herbs are used, the amount should be much less, as they are stronger and more concentrated than the fresh. One teaspoon of the dried or one tablespoon of the fresh herbs is a good rule to follow.

SOUP BAGS: The following directions for making soup bags are taken from Mrs. Hollis Webster's excellent *Bulletin on Herbs*.

Make small cheesecloth bags about 2 in. square and fill with a bouquet of dried herbs. The quantity given in the following recipes will fill three bags, and in each is enough seasoning for about two quarts of liquid. The bags are dropped into the boiling soup toward the end of cooking, and should not be left in more than an hour or according to taste. Long cooking makes herbs bitter and destroys the fine essence of distinction between the different kinds in the 'bouquet.' The little sack of herbs should not be used again, though it often is.

FOR CONSOMME

¼ tsp. peppercorns	5 tsp. parsley
3 cloves (1 in each bag)	½ tsp. savory
2 tsp. thyme	3 Tbs. celery
1 tsp. marjoram	

FOR TOMATO SOUP

1 small bay leaf	1 tsp. basil
3 cloves (1 in each bag)	2 Tbs. celery
1 tsp. thyme	1 Tbs. parsley

FOR FISH STOCK

(or to boil with salmon, halibut, etc.)

1 small bay leaf	3 peppercorns
½ tsp. sage	2 Tbs. celery
1 tsp. savory	¼ tsp. basil
3 cloves (1 in each bag)	½ tsp. fennel

FOR FLAVORING MEAT GRAVIES, BEEF STOCK, AND BAKED LIVER

1 tsp. dried parsley	¼ tsp. bay leaf
1 tsp. dried thyme	2 tsp. dried celery (leaf and
1 tsp. dried marjoram	stem tips or the grated
¼ tsp. dried sage	root of this herb)
½ tsp. savory	

AROMATIC SEASONING

1 oz. nutmeg	3 oz. basil
1 oz. mace	3 oz. marjoram
2 oz. cloves	2 oz. winter savory
2 oz. peppercorns	3 oz. thyme
1 oz. dried bay leaves	½ oz. cayenne pepper
2 cloves of garlic	½ oz. grated lemon peel

All these ingredients must be well pulverized in a mortar and sifted through a fine wire sieve. Put in dry corked bottles for use.

SOUPS

Soups need no introduction: they are themselves the introduction to the meal of the day and, indeed, in European peasant cookery, they often constitute the main dish of the main meal, combining in one glorious mixture soup, meat, potatoes, and green vegetables — and sometimes fish. Herbs can and do go into most of these recipes either as a bouquet in the foundation bouillon, or as fine herbs added at the last. If in the following pages the hearty type of vegetable or leguminous soup seems to predominate, try any one of them as a 'meal in itself.' Served in a tureen or casserole on the table, followed by a green salad or fruit and cheese, it will be found adequate and satisfying, and if there is any left over it can be reheated the next day in the same dish.

RECIPES

BLACK BEAN SOUP

2 cups black beans	2 peppercorns
2 qts. water	2 cloves
Ham bone or ¼ lb. salt pork	2 sprigs thyme (or 1 bay leaf)
2 stalks celery	1 onion

Soak beans overnight, drain and cook with the water, ham bone, and other ingredients until soft enough to rub through a coarse strainer (about 8 hours). Reheat; add 2 Tbs. sherry or Marsala wine to each soup plate, 1 slice hard-boiled egg, and 1 slice lemon.

BOHEMIAN VEGETABLE SOUP

2 Tbs. of barley boiled 1 hour in	2 small onions
2 qts. of water	1 medium potato
2 or 3 small carrots	4 stalks of celery
	1 turnip

All vegetables are put through the meat grinder, then put into the barley water and boiled slowly. Pepper and salt to taste. Then thicken with 2 Tbs. flour, slightly burnt and cooked with 3 Tbs. of melted butter. Boil up and serve.

BORSTCH (BEET), LITTLE RUSSIA

2 large boiled beets	Juice of 1 lemon
1 grated raw beet	1 tsp. sugar
1 qt. white stock	1 cup whipped cream

Grate the boiled beets and add to stock with the lemon juice and sugar; simmer for 5 minutes, then add the juice of the grated raw beet, squeezed through a cheesecloth: scald and stir in whipped cream. Serve *very hot* or chilled.

CARROT SOUP (POTAGE CRÉCY)

2 bunches carrots	4 Tbs. butter
1 onion	1 tsp. salt
1 head celery	Pepper
Parsley	3 cups stock
Thyme	2 cups milk

Slice carrots, onion, and celery and cook in butter with herbs slowly for a half hour, stirring occasionally. Add stock and seasoning and cook 1 hour; then strain into hot milk. Bind with 1 Tbs. butter cooked with 1 Tbs. flour.

CARROT-POTATO SOUP

4 medium potatoes	Herb combination:
3 large carrots	2 sprigs summer savory
2 Tbs. butter	2 sprigs parsley
1 Tbs. flour	2 sprigs thyme
3½ cups milk	2 sage leaves
1 tsp. salt	
Pepper	

Cook potatoes and carrots in water until tender. Rub through a fine sieve. Blend butter and flour, add milk and the potato-carrot mixture. Tie fresh herb combination with piece of white string and place in soup. Season with salt and pepper and heat slowly; cook 5 minutes and remove herb bouquet. Serve at once.

CELERY STOCK

2 bunches of celery, or	1½ qts. water
6 to 8 outside stalks	1 tsp. salt
(with leaves)	4 peppercorns
1 small onion, sliced	2 cloves
4 sprigs parsley	1 blade mace

Cut up celery and cook slowly with other ingredients for several hours. Strain and add salt.

Add other vegetables to the above — carrots, turnips, or any left-overs — and you will have a good vegetable stock which will keep several days on ice.

For a plain celery broth, add to the celery stock an equal amount of chicken or veal stock, a little minced celery, and a teaspoon of cream to each soup plate. This may be served chilled in cups.

CHERVIL SOUP

1 lb. mixed soup veg-	2 egg yolks
etables and greens	2 Tbs. sour cream
1 Tbs. butter	⅓ cup chervil, cleaned
1 Tbs. flour	and chopped
1 qt. weak stock (or	1 Tbs. butter
1 bouillon cube and	Salt
1 qt. boiling water)	

Clean greens. Cut in small pieces and sauté in fat 2 minutes. Add flour and mix. Add stock, salt; partially cover and simmer 1 hour. Rub through sieve. Add small amount to egg yolks and then stir into remaining hot soup Add sour cream and butter and heat almost to boiling. Add chervil and serve at once.

CREAM OF FINOCCHIO (FENNEL)

1 large stalk finocchio
   (or 4 stalks of the common fennel)
2 cups chicken stock
½ small onion, sliced
2 cups milk

1 Tbs. butter
1 Tbs. flour
1 tsp. salt
⅛ tsp. pepper
Cream

Remove tops, cut up bulb and stalks; cook with onion in stock until soft. Add milk and press through coarse strainer. Cook butter and flour together; add soup and seasoning. Add ¼ cup cream and sprinkle with finely minced fennel leaves. This may also have one or two egg yolks stirred with the cream added as the soup is taken off the fire.

HERB SOUPS

No. 1 (stock)

4 lbs. rump beef
5 qts. cold water
2 tsp. salt
3 medium onions
2 carrots, scraped

1 turnip, quartered
1 parsnip, cut in strips
1 small head of celery, sliced
Cloves
Herb bouquet

Wipe beef. Cover with cold water. Bring to boiling point and skim carefully. Simmer 2 hours. Add salt and vegetables. Stick an onion full of cloves; add herb bouquet and simmer gently 1 hour. Remove vegetables and meat. Season to taste. Serve in a separate dish.

HERB BOUQUET: thyme, winter savory, and fennel is a good soup combination.

No. 2. HERB SOUP

3 Tbs. butter
1 head lettuce, shredded
1 small bunch watercress,
   cut fine
1 tsp. chervil, minced
1 tsp. parsley, minced

6 cups chicken stock
½ cup cream
1 egg yolk
Salt
Pepper

Cook lettuce and watercress in the butter for 5 minutes,

being careful not to brown the herbs. Add stock and seasoning to taste. Cook a half hour, then add chervil and parsley and cream mixed with egg yolk. Stir until heated but do not boil.

No. 3 (with sorrel and spinach)

1 cup finely shredded spinach	3 tsp. salt
½ cup shredded sorrel	4 Tbs. butter
4 medium potatoes	2 qts. boiling water
1 leek	1 Tbs. minced chervil
1 head lettuce	

Use fresh sorrel, spinach, and inside leaves of lettuce; wash and shred, discarding tough midribs. Cut leek into thin slices; cook in butter 15 minutes, being careful not to brown. Add potatoes, salt, and boiling water; boil quickly; reduce heat and boil gently for 1 hour. Crush the potatoes with a fork, add the chervil, and simmer 5 minutes longer. Turn into a soup tureen, add fried croutons, and serve.

If preferred the soup may be rubbed through a purée sieve, returned to the fire, and when boiling hot be poured onto the yolks of 2 eggs mixed with 2 Tbs. milk.

This soup may be varied indefinitely. Any number of green vegetables can be used, care being taken to use only a small quantity of those of pronounced flavor.

No. 4 (with vegetables)

3 heads lettuce	3 sprigs tarragon
4 stalks celery	3 sprigs thyme
2 onions	2 egg yolks
1 handful chervil	½ cup cream
1 handful sorrel	Salt
1 qt. water	Pepper

Shred the lettuce, cut up celery, onions, sorrel, and chervil, and boil in water with thyme till well stewed. Strain off the herbs a half hour before dinner; add tarragon and let the soup cool, then add cream stirred in egg yolks. Stir well, and put it on the fire to heat but do not let boil.

LEEK SOUP

4 leeks	1 cup heavy cream
1 medium onion	Chives, finely chopped
1 Tbs. unsalted butter	Salt
1 qt. white stock	Pepper

Cut up the white part of leeks with the onion and cook in butter until yellow. Add stock and boil for 40 minutes. Strain twice through a muslin cloth or very fine wire strainer. Season and stir in cream and serve hot with chives mixed in. This may also be served cold.

LEEK AND POTATO SOUP ('VICHYSOISSE')

4 leeks, sliced	2 cups hot milk
1 medium-sized onion, sliced	1 cup heavy cream
2 medium-sized potatoes, sliced	Salt
4 Tbs. sweet butter	Minced chives
1 qt. white stock or boiling water	

Cook leeks and onion in butter until yellow, add potatoes, ½ tsp. salt, and stock or water. Boil 30 minutes or until thoroughly soft, mash through strainer; add hot milk, season to taste, and strain again through fine muslin. Reheat, add the cream, and sprinkle with finely chopped chives on top of each portion. Serve ice cold. This is known as 'Vichysoisse,' and the cream should not be added until after the soup has been thoroughly chilled in a bowl of cracked ice.

GREEN LEEK SOUP

Tops of 4 leeks	1 strip bacon
1 lb. spinach	Herb bouquet
1 cup green peas	(parsley, thyme, celery leaves)
6 cups water	1 cup cream
1 onion, chopped	1 tsp. salt

Cook leek tops, spinach, and peas in water with salt. Fry onion and bacon 2 or 3 minutes, and add with herb bouquet to the soup mixture as it comes to a boil. Let simmer for about 1½ hours; press through strainer; add more water if necessary, and just before serving add the cream. Serve with croutons.

LENTIL SOUP, NO. 1

2 cups lentils	1 bay leaf
2 qts. stock	A few celery leaves
4 Tbs. butter	1 sprig parsley
1 onion, sliced	1 sprig thyme
Salt	Frankfurter sausages
Pepper	

Soak lentils in cold water overnight. Strain and wash them again, then put them in an earthen pot with stock and simmer for 1½ hours. Fry onion, parsley, celery leaves, thyme, and bay leaf in butter. Add these to the lentils and simmer for another half hour. Rub through sieve and bring to a boil. Season and serve with slices of Frankfurter sausages added 10 minutes before taking the soup off the fire.

LENTIL SOUP, NO. 2

2 cups lentils	6 Tbs. butter
2 carrots	1 Tbs. flour
1 white turnip	2 cloves
2 onions	1 Tbs. chopped parsley
1 qt. stock	½ tsp. chives
¼ lb. mushrooms	A little basil
	Salt

Put the lentils in a saucepan with the chopped onions, turnip, and carrots, which have been slightly fried in butter first. Remove the lentils when cooked; drain and put them into a casserole with 4 Tbs. butter, a little onion, some stock, cloves, herbs, mushrooms, and seasoning.

Thicken the stock with 1 Tbs. butter and 1 Tbs. flour

browned, and let the whole simmer till cooked. Crush it all into a purée, add the carrot and turnip and a little more stock. Serve with fried croutons.

LENTIL SOUP, NO. 3

1 cup lentils	1 bunch parsley
2 anchovies	A little sage
3 cups stock	Salt
½ cup olive oil	

Put lentils, well cleaned and dry, into boiling water in an earthen pot. Be careful to remove those which float to the surface. Leave the rest to cook until they are quite soft; then take them out and drain them.

Meanwhile mix anchovies, parsley, and sage with some oil in a saucepan. When well browned put in the lentils. Stir well, add more oil, and cook over a slow fire, stirring from time to time. When ready, mix in stock; season and serve with croutons.

LENTIL SOUP, NO. 4

(with sorrel)

2 cups lentils	1 carrot, sliced
3 qts. water	1 onion, sliced
2 handfuls sorrel	2 leeks, sliced
½ lb. lean salt pork	1 raw potato, sliced
2 Tbs. butter	2 stalks celery, sliced
1 tsp. salt	1 sprig chervil
½ tsp. pepper	

Soak lentils in cold water 4 hours. Drain and place in saucepan with water. Add salt pork, vegetables, chervil, and seasoning; cover and cook slowly for 1½ hours.

Prepare sorrel, stripping leaves from stalks; chop fine and cook in butter. Strain soup through a fine sieve into the sorrel, boil 5 minutes, and serve with croutons.

LETTUCE SOUP

1 head lettuce, chopped fine	1 small white onion
1 pt. young green peas, with pods	Blanched leaves of 2 heads celery
	1 sprig thyme
4 boiled potatoes	½ cup cream
1½ qts. consommé	Salt

Bring consommé to boiling; add the potatoes, which have been coarsely mashed, the celery, lettuce, thyme, onion, and green peas. Boil for 1½ hours, put through coarse strainer; season; add cream and serve with croutons.

MINESTRONE ALLA NAPOLITANA

1 cabbage	¼ lb. salt pork
2 carrots, sliced	1½ qts. stock
2 onions, sliced	½ cup rice (or macaroni)
2 leeks, sliced	Salt
1 stalk celery, sliced	Pepper
2 turnips, sliced	French roll

Mince the salt pork and try out in saucepan; add onions and vegetables and shredded cabbage which has been soaked in salted water for a half hour. Fry all together, moisten with hot bouillon, and stew gently until all the vegetables are done. Boil rice or macaroni cut into short pieces; add to the contents of saucepan and continue to simmer until done. Season with salt and pepper.

Put slices of toasted French roll in bottom of a tureen and pour the minestrone over them. Serve very hot. It should be thick enough to be eaten with a fork as well as a spoon

ONION SOUP
(three versions)

No. 1. With stock, any kind, rather thin.

4 large onions (or 1 to each serving)	Salt
1 qt. stock — add 1 cup for each extra portion	Black pepper, freshly ground
4 Tbs. butter — add 1 Tbs. for each extra portion	Thick slices or crusts of French, Italian, or Vienna bread
	Parmesan cheese

Slice the onions in rings and fry in butter until light brown, stirring constantly. Add stock and simmer for 15 to 25 minutes. If liquid has materially reduced, add enough boiling water for the required amount. Salt and pepper to taste. Have ready slices of well-toasted bread, place them in soup plates and cover with onion, spooned out in equal portions; sprinkle a little grated cheese over each one, then pour in the soup and serve with more grated cheese passed at the table.

No. 2. With stock, milk, and egg yolks. A hearty version and a complete meal in itself. Need be followed only by a green salad or fruit.

4 large onions (or 1 to each portion)	2 egg yolks
1 qt. thin stock, any kind	Salt
4 Tbs. butter	Black pepper
½ cup thin cream or rich milk	2 Tbs. grated Parmesan cheese

Slice and fry onions in butter until yellow, stirring constantly. Drain off butter and add stock (any kind); simmer about 20 minutes. Season with salt and freshly ground pepper and remove to hot casserole in which it is to be served. Mix egg yolks with cream and stir in hot soup. Add Parmesan cheese, stirring well.

Place 1 or 2 pieces well-toasted French bread in each soup plate; put a spoonful of onions on each piece and then a ladleful of soup. Pass more grated Parmesan cheese.

No. 3. With boiling water. This version is less nutritious but more delicate, and may be followed by the usual dinner.

'A la Stanislas'

(Translated and adapted from a French
recipe contributed by Helmut Ripperger)

Crust from loaf of French or Vienna bread	4 to 5 cups boiling water
	Salt
3 large onions	Black pepper, freshly ground
3 Tbs. sweet butter	

Remove crust from the top of the loaf of bread and break into medium-sized pieces. Place on a baking sheet in the oven and crisp them, turning over several times; then spread with butter and place them under the broiler. When lightly toasted set aside on a plate until needed. Dice the onions and fry in 3 Tbs. of butter until light brown, stirring constantly; then add the crusts. Stir continually until the onion is brown. When it has taken on enough color, moisten with the boiling water, scraping with a spoon to loosen the mixture from the casserole. Then add the seasoning to taste and the rest of the boiling water. Let it simmer at least a quarter hour. Serve in the casserole and pass grated Parmesan cheese.

PARSLEY SOUP

3 cups boiling water or stock (half milk may be used)	1 egg yolk
	½ cup cream
1 Tbs. butter	Salt
3 Tbs. chopped parsley	Pepper
1 clove garlic	

Fry parsley in butter; add stock and garlic and bring to boil. Take out garlic. Stir egg yolk in cream and add to soup just before serving. Serve with croutons fried in butter or toasted French bread.

PEA SOUPS

FRESH GREEN PEA

2 cups green peas	1 Tbs. butter
Pea-pods	1 Tbs. flour
1 small head lettuce, shredded	1 cup cream
	Herb bouquet of mint or
3 sprigs parsley	Thyme and celery leaves or
2 medium onions, chopped	Soup bag of dried herbs
1 qt. water	1 tsp. salt
1 Tbs. sugar	½ tsp. pepper

Wash pods, cut up into small pieces, and put in a saucepan with the onions, lettuce, parsley, sugar, and herbs; cover with cold water, boil up once, and simmer gently till the shells are soft. Add salt and pepper. Drain off liquor into a bowl and save. Remove herb bouquet from peas and press through a sieve into strained liquor.

Put the shelled peas into a clean saucepan; add contents of the bowl; boil until peas are soft, then pass all through a fine strainer. Cook butter and flour together; add soup and cook until it thickens slightly and stir in heated cream before serving. Serve with fried croutons.

For a richer purée, add 2 egg yolks stirred into the cream.

PEA-POD

2 qts. sugar peas or 'mange-tout'	1 egg yolk
	1 cup cream
2 medium potatoes	1 Tbs. sugar
1 onion, cut up	1 tsp. salt
1 sprig thyme	1 Tbs. butter

String and wash well the pods and put in saucepan with potatoes and onion and cold water to cover. Add sugar and thyme. Boil hard until potatoes are soft, then press through a coarse sieve. Return to saucepan; bring to a boil; add salt and pour over egg yolk mixed with cream. Add fresh butter and serve with fried croutons.

GREEN SPLIT PEA

2 cups green split peas
1 qt. water
1 onion, chopped
1 stalk celery
¼ lb. salt pork
2 sprigs thyme (or ½ tsp. dried)

2 cups milk
1 Tbs. butter
1 Tbs. flour
Salt
Pepper

Soak peas overnight, drain, and cook in water with pork and other ingredients. Cook until soft enough to pass through sieve. Add milk and seasoning, and thicken with butter and flour cooked together. Boil up once and serve with croutons.

POTAGE VERT PRÉ

2 cups green split peas
2 cups fresh sorrel leaves
1 carrot, sliced
1 onion, sliced
2 branches celery
2 leeks
2 raw potatoes, peeled and sliced
Ham bone

3 qts. water
2 sprigs parsley
2 tsp. salt
½ tsp. pepper
1 tsp. sugar
3 Tbs. cooked fresh green peas
1 Tbs. butter
2 sprigs chervil, minced

Soak split peas overnight. Drain and put in saucepan with the water and all the vegetables except the fresh green peas and chervil. Add ham bone and seasoning and boil 1½ hours, stirring occasionally. Press soup through strainer, add cooked green peas, chervil, and by little bits the butter. Mix well; bring to the boil and serve with croutons or toasted French bread.

YELLOW SPLIT PEA

2 cups yellow split peas	**1** ham bone (or ¼ lb. salt pork)
2 qts. water	**2** sprigs summer savory
2 white onions, cut in quarters	Salt
2 stalks celery (or dried celery leaves)	Pepper

Soak peas overnight. Drain and add water, celery, onion, and ham bone. Cook until peas are soft enough to press through coarse strainer. Season and reheat in casserole with summer savory. Remove savory and serve in casserole.

POTAGE BONNE FEMME

1 bunch sorrel	**2** Tbs. flour
1 handful purslane or	**2** cups water
1 small head lettuce	**2** cups milk
2 medium onions, chopped	**1** egg
2 Tbs. minced chervil	Salt
6 Tbs. butter	Sugar

Fry onions in 4 Tbs. butter for 5 minutes, but do not brown them. Shred lettuce or purslane and sorrel leaves and add to onions, with chervil and seasoning. Stir all together on the fire for 5 minutes and then add flour. Let this cook for another 5 minutes, and then gradually pour in milk and water. Bring gently to the boil and let simmer for a quarter hour.

Beat egg, add 2 Tbs. butter, and pour a little of the hot soup into the cup with the egg to melt butter. Place 3 or 4 slices toasted French bread in the soup tureen, pour soup on the bread, and then stir in the egg mixture.

POTAGE SANTÉ

½ lb. mealy potatoes	**2** egg yolks
1 handful sorrel	**1** cup cream
2 leeks	Salt
5 cups boiling water	Pepper
4 Tbs. butter	

Cut potatoes into small pieces and cook in 2 Tbs. butter

with the leeks cut into thin slices. Add seasoning and cook for a few minutes, then add boiling water. Boil quickly, and when the vegetables are cooked mash them through a strainer.

Wash and chop the sorrel and cook in 2 Tbs. butter. Combine with the purée of vegetables, bring to a boil, and let simmer 20 minutes. Stir in at the last minute the egg yolks mixed with the cream; stir well and serve at once.

ROSEMARY SOUP

1 Tbs. dried rosemary	3 Tbs. butter
(or 2 Tbs. fresh)	1 egg yolk
1 head lettuce	½ cup cream
1 cup sorrel	Salt
1 cup watercress	Pepper
1½ qts. chicken stock, or half water	

Cook in butter for about 5 minutes the rosemary, lettuce, sorrel, and watercress, all shredded or cut fine. Add stock and simmer a half hour. Mix the egg yolk with the cream and stir into the mixture just before taking off the fire. Add seasoning and serve immediately.

SORREL SOUP

2 bunches sorrel	2 or 3 egg yolks, stirred into
4 Tbs. butter	1 cup cream (or milk)
2 cups boiling water	Salt
(or chicken stock)	Pepper
1 tsp. flour	

Wash and dry the sorrel. Chop it fine and cook in butter until it becomes a pulp. Sprinkle in flour, salt, and pepper to taste; add chicken stock or boiling water. When it boils add the egg yolks mixed with the cream (or milk). Serve with croutons or toasted Italian bread.

SPINACH SOUP

1 lb. spinach (cooked and put through a sieve)	2 Tbs. minced chervil
2 cups chicken or beef stock	1 cup cream
1 cup boiling water	Nutmeg
1 onion, grated	Salt
	Pepper

Boil spinach, chervil, onion, stock, and boiling water together 5 minutes; season with salt, pepper, and a grating of nutmeg. Bind with 1 Tbs. flour cooked with 1 Tbs. butter. Just before serving add the cream.

TOMATO SOUPS

No. 1

4 large tomatoes (or 1 large can)	1 bay leaf or sprig thyme
2 cups stock (or water)	2 sprigs basil
1 large onion, sliced	1 stalk celery cut up (or celery leaves)
1 Tbs. butter	½ tsp. salt
1 Tbs. flour	4 peppercorns
	1 clove

Simmer tomatoes with herbs, stock, peppercorns, and cloves about 40 minutes. Fry the onion in the butter but do not brown. Add flour and cook 5 minutes, stirring well. Dilute with a little of the soup; add salt and the rest of the tomato mixture. Bring to a boil, strain, and serve with fried croutons.

No. 2 (with milk)

1 can (or 4 cups) tomatoes	2 or 3 sprigs basil
2 cups hot milk	1 Tbs. butter
1 onion	1 Tbs. flour
1 bay leaf	1 tsp. salt
2 sprigs thyme	A little pepper
	½ cup cream

Cook the tomatoes for 1 hour with the onion and herbs. Put through a very fine strainer. Cook the butter and flour together; add hot milk and strained tomatoes. Season and cook in double boiler 2 or 3 minutes, add cream. Serve with a bit of basil on each plate.

No. 3. Spanish Soup

3 Tbs. red and green peppers	1 drop Tabasco sauce
2 cups tomatoes	2 sprigs basil
3 cups stock	Salt
2 Tbs. butter	Paprika
2 Tbs. flour	½ cup macaroni

Chop the peppers and cook in butter for 5 minutes. Add the stock, basil, and tomatoes. Cover and simmer gently for 20 minutes. Strain and season, adding the macaroni, cooked and cut into rings.

TURKEY BISQUE

Turkey carcass	2 tsp. salt
1 cup chopped celery	5 peppercorns
1 cup oysters (in their liquor)	Parsley
½ cup uncooked rice	1 bay leaf
6 cups hot water	1 cup hot cream

Break the turkey into pieces and put into soup kettle with the hot water; cover and simmer gently 1 hour. Then add the celery, parsley, bay leaf, peppercorns, salt, and uncooked rice. Scald the oysters in their liquor, chop them fine, and add them with the liquor to the soup. Simmer until the rice is tender, then strain the soup through a coarse sieve, pressing through as much of the rice and oysters as possible. Return to the fire, add the hot cream, and beat the soup with a Dover beater.

WATERCRESS SOUP

2 bunches watercress	3 Tbs. butter
2 medium potatoes	¼ cup cream
1 qt. stock	1 egg yolk
1 onion minced	Salt
1 bay leaf	Pepper
1 sprig thyme	Paprika

Wash the watercress carefully, then chop fine. Peel and dice the potatoes. Melt the butter in a deep skillet; add the watercress and the onion, bay leaf, and thyme. When the cress is limp, add the potatoes and cover with the stock (canned chicken soup). Simmer with the egg yolk stirred into the cream. Serve at once, garnished with chopped watercress and parsley.

CHAPTER III

FISH

LIST OF RECIPES

The two herbs most often used in cooking fish are perhaps
basil and fennel, but dill, thyme, and bay leaf are indispensable, and the ever useful clove of garlic must not be
forgotten! In preparing fish, as in other meats, the choice
of herbs is largely a matter of individual taste, and the cook
should be encouraged to experiment and vary the combinations.

Directions for boiling fish usually call for court bouillon.
A simple one may be made merely by adding lemon, onion,

and herbs, such as basil or thyme, to the water in which the fish is to be cooked. The following is a more elaborate recipe:

COURT BOUILLON

2 stalks celery, cut in small pieces	6 peppercorns
1 carrot, cut up	2 cloves
1 onion, cut up	1 clove garlic
2 sprigs parsley	1 Tbs. salt
1 sprig thyme	1 Tbs. lemon juice
1 bay leaf	2 qts. water
	1 cup white wine

Put the water in a large kettle with all the ingredients and boil 15 or 20 minutes. After the fish has been boiled the liquid should be strained and kept to use for fish sauces.

When broiling any kind of fish, make an herb butter and spread half on one side of the fish, broil, turn over, spread the rest on the other side, and finish broiling.

HERB BUTTER

¼ cup soft butter	⅛ tsp. pepper
½ tsp. salt	1½ Tbs. minced herbs

Combine all, working well with a fork until thoroughly mixed.

Combinations of herbs:

> Basil, chives, and parsley
> Dill and parsley
> Fennel, chervil, and chives

RECIPES

BOUILLABAISSE NO. 1

1½ lbs. of any firm white fish
(at least 2 varieties such as
carp, eel, rock cod or halibut)
½ lb. shrimps, crab or other
shell fish
6 onions, cut up
1 clove garlic
½ cup olive oil
2 cups white wine
Boiling water
1 Tbs. minced parsley

1 sprig thyme
1 bay leaf
2 cloves
4 peppercorns
1½ tsp. salt
1 Tbs. lemon juice
Rind of ½ lemon
1 tsp. turmeric
A little saffron, dissolved in
hot stock

Put in a casserole the oil, garlic, onions, bay leaf, and thyme and cook 15 minutes. Remove the garlic and put in the fish; add wine and enough boiling water to cover. Bring quickly to a boil; add rest of ingredients and cook about a half hour or until fish is done. If the liquid cooks away too much, add more boiling water, as there should be plenty of bouillon. Serve in soup plates with pieces of toasted French bread.

BOUILLABAISSE NO. 2 (CREOLE)

6 slices red snapper
6 slices redfish
2 doz. small shrimps
2 cups white wine
4 fresh tomatoes, cut in pieces
(or ½ can)
3 medium onions, chopped
3 cloves garlic
2 bay leaves

3 sprigs thyme
3 sprigs parsley
¼ tsp. allspice
⅛ tsp. saffron
½ lemon, cut in thin slices
2 Tbs. olive oil
Cayenne pepper
Salt
Pepper

Make a bouillon by cooking the head and tail of the red snapper in 1½ qts. of water with an herb bouquet (bay leaf, parsley, and thyme), 1 onion, and 2 slices of lemon until reduced one-half. Strain and cook the shrimps in the bouillon. Set aside until needed.

Rub fish slices well with salt and pepper. Mince garlic and herbs very fine and mix with allspice; rub each slice of fish with this mixture till well permeated. Heat olive oil in a large frying-pan; add the onions, then lay in the slices of fish in the pan side by side and cover. Let cook slowly 10 minutes, turning fish over once so both sides will be cooked. Take out the slices of fish and set aside to keep hot. Pour wine into the pan, stirring well. Add tomatoes and the lemon slices and pour over the liquor in which the fish was cooked. Season with salt, pepper, and cayenne and boil until reduced one-half. Lay in the fish slice by slice and the shrimps; bring to a boil and let cook 5 minutes. Mince the saffron and soak this in a little of the hot sauce, then spread it over the fish slices.

Toast slices of bread and fry in butter. Drain on paper and arrange on a platter. Put each slice of fish on a piece of toast and pour over the sauce with the shrimps.

CHOWDER

(*New England Fish Chowder*)

3 lbs. fresh cod or haddock	1 Tbs. celery, minced
2 cups parboiled potatoes cut in slices	1 Tbs. carrot, minced
4 cups milk	1 Tbs. fresh sage, minced
1 large onion, sliced	1 sprig thyme
2 Tbs. butter	2 tsp. salt
1 Tbs. flour	Pepper
3 Tbs. minced salt pork	Common crackers
	Worcestershire sauce

Cut off head and tail together with backbone and cook in 2 cups cold water about 20 minutes. Try out salt pork, add onion, and fry; then add potatoes and fish stock and cook 5 minutes. Add the fish cut in pieces, cover, and cook ten minutes. Add carrot, celery, herbs, seasoning, and hot milk. Simmer 5 minutes, thicken with butter and flour cooked together, add a dash of Worcestershire sauce, and serve in large tureen with crackers split and toasted floating in soup.

DEVILLED CRAB

1 lb. crab meat	1 tsp. minced parsley
1 cup cold milk	1 tsp. mustard
¼ cup cream	½ tsp. salt
½ medium onion, chopped	½ saltspoon nutmeg
½ clove garlic, chopped	½ saltspoon cayenne pepper
2 Tbs. butter	2 egg yolks
2 Tbs. flour	4 Tbs. bread crumbs
1 Tbs. Worcestershire sauce	

Mix milk, cream, parsley, Worcestershire sauce, nutmeg, mustard, salt, and cayenne pepper in saucepan and boil 5 minutes, stirring constantly. Cook onion in butter until golden brown; then add flour, mixing well with a wooden spoon. Pour contents of other pan into this and simmer 5 minutes. Add egg yolks, stirring briskly till thickened. Add crab meat; stir 2 minutes.

Pour onto a flat dish and cool. Fill 6 medium-sized crab shells with mixture. Smooth with knife blade. Divide equally the devilled butter on top and spread the bread crumbs over it. Arrange in baking-dish and bake in hot oven 10 minutes. Decorate with minced parsley on lemon slices.

Devilled Butter

2 Tbs. butter	1 saltspoon salt
2 saltspoons mustard	½ saltspoon cayenne pepper
1 tsp. tarragon vinegar	1 egg yolk
1 tsp. Worcestershire sauce	1 tsp. minced tarragon

Mix thoroughly.

FISH À LA PROVENÇAL

2 lbs. halibut (or any other fish), cut in slices 1 inch thick	1 clove garlic
4 Tbs. olive oil	Saffron, allspice, mace
1 Tbs. minced parsley	Salt
1 Tbs. minced shallot	Paprika
1 Tbs. minced chives	1 cup boiling water
1 Tbs. minced basil	2 egg yolks
	Lemon juice

Clean and wipe dry the slices of fish. Pour the olive oil into a shallow casserole; add the minced herbs and the clove of garlic and bring to boiling point. Sprinkle fish with allspice, mace, and a pinch of saffron.

Turn over in the oil two or three times, then add salt and paprika. Take out garlic and add a cup of boiling water. Simmer slowly until done. Beat the egg yolks with a little lemon juice. Pour some of the fish broth into it. Then stir all into the casserole and as soon as sauce thickens slightly, serve.

HALIBUT
(baked with fine herbs)

1½ lbs. halibut (in 1 piece)	1 tsp. minced parsley
2 qts. court bouillon	1 tsp. minced basil
1 Tbs. butter	2 Tbs. grated Parmesan cheese
1 Tbs. flour	

Cook the halibut in court bouillon (page 34). Remove and place in shallow casserole. Cook the butter and flour together, add 2 cups stock in which fish was cooked, seasoning, and 1 Tbs. cheese. Cook until slightly thickened. Pour over fish and add the rest of the cheese, basil, and parsley. Bake in a hot oven 5 minutes.

LOBSTER NEWBURG

2 cups lobster meat	½ cup sherry
3 hard-boiled eggs	1 tsp. minced tarragon
4 Tbs. butter	Salt
1 Tbs. flour	Pepper
1 cup cream	

Press egg whites through a coarse sieve. Mash egg yolks

and moisten with a little cream. Rub flour into butter until smooth; melt in saucepan, add lobster, egg yolks and whites, and the rest of the cream. Season. Stir until well heated; whip in the sherry; add salt and dust thickly with paprika, adding minced tarragon at the last.

DEVILLED LOBSTER (THERMIDOR)

3 cups lobster meat	1 tsp. salt
6 mushrooms, chopped	½ tsp. mustard
1 onion, minced	1 saltspoon cayenne pepper
2 Tbs. butter	1 saltspoon nutmeg
1 Tbs. flour	2 egg yolks
1½ cups hot milk	4 Tbs. bread crumbs
1 Tbs. Worcestershire sauce	

Cut up the lobster meat into small pieces. Add mushrooms, which have been sautéed 3 minutes in butter. Cook onions in butter; add flour, stirring well, and milk. Stir until it boils, then put in lobster and mushrooms. Add seasoning and cook a few minutes. Thicken with egg yolks and cook 5 minutes, stirring constantly.

Let cool and fill 6 half lobster shells, smoothing with knife. Divide equally the devilled butter (p. 37) on top and spread over the bread crumbs. Arrange in baking-pan and bake in hot oven 10 minutes. Decorate with minced parsley on lemon slices.

BROILED MACKEREL, SALMON, OR HALIBUT STEAKS
(with fine herbs)

Prepare fish for broiling, and before putting under fire spread with a mixture of butter and fine herbs, using half the entire amount. Broil one side, turn over, and spread with the remaining half.

Herb Butter Mixture

¼ cup soft butter	1½ Tbs. minced herbs (basil, parsley,
½ tsp. salt	and chives, or dill and parsley, or
1 saltspoon pepper	fennel, chervil, and chives)

MACKEREl
(with fennel)

Split a 2-lb. mackerel and remove backbone. Place in saucepan with enough cold water to cover; add 2 slices lemon and 2 Tbs. chopped green fennel. Let it come to a boil, add 1 tsp. salt, and simmer gently for 15 minutes. Take out and drain; arrange on dish and pour over sauce.

Fennel Sauce

Add to ½ cup mayonnaise 1 Tbs. thin cream and 1 tsp. finely minced fennel.

Or, use the water in which fish was cooked; thicken it with 1 Tbs. butter and 1 Tbs. flour, cooked together; add 1 tsp. lemon juice, salt and pepper, and 1 Tbs. chopped fennel.

OYSTERS
(baked with fine herbs)

> 6 oysters to a portion
> Freezing salt
> Bacon (1 slice to each portion)
> Chives
> Parsley
> Chervil
> Thyme

Fill layer-cake tins with freezing salt and put in a hot oven until the salt is thoroughly heated. Half-sink 8 oysters on the half shell in the salt of each tin and season.

Run through a meat grinder bacon, with chives, parsley, chervil, and a very little fresh thyme, and then pound until the mixture becomes a paste. Dot the paste over the oysters, and place in a very hot oven (500° F.) until the oysters curl up at the edges. Serve in the tins in which baked, with a little bowl of sauce at each plate.

Sauce

1 Tbs. butter to each portion	A dash of horseradish
Lemon juice	Salt, pepper
Worcestershire sauce	A dash of Tabasco

Melt butter in a double boiler and add seasoning. Each oyster is dipped in the sauce as eaten.

OYSTERS À L'ANCIEN

6 oysters to a portion	Minced parsley
(Cape Cod or Buzzards Bay)	Minced chives
Bacon	Salt
Butter	Paprika

Arrange oysters on the half shell on baking-sheet. Dot each with a dab of butter, parsley, chives, salt and paprika, and a small piece of thinly sliced bacon, cut in squares with a scissors. Place under broiler long enough to crisp the bacon and serve at once.

SALMON
(with sauce hollandaise and tarragon)

Boil a 3-lb. piece of salmon in court bouillon (page 34). Serve with Hollandaise sauce flavored with tarragon vinegar and minced fresh tarragon, added after it is cooked.

SALMON
(with green mayonnaise)

Boil a 2-lb. or 3-lb. piece of salmon in court bouillon (page 34). Chill and serve with green mayonnaise sauce. It may be masked with the mayonnaise or the mayonnaise passed separately.

Green Mayonnaise

½ pt. plain mayonnaise	1 Tbs. chervil
1 Tbs. parsley	1 Tbs. minced tarragon
1 Tbs. watercress	Salt

Boil parsley, watercress, and chervil in salted water for

7 minutes; drain it and press through a fine sieve into the mayonnaise, beating well. Add minced fresh tarragon.

FILET OF SOLE
(with white wine — 'sole au vin blanc')

6 filets	Flour
2 Tbs. butter	Parmesan cheese
½ cup dry white wine	Herb bouquet (thyme, parsley,
1 tsp. minced onion	celery leaves)
¼ lb. mushrooms, sliced	Salt
½ cup thick cream	Pepper

Sauté filets in butter, remove from saucepan, and place in casserole. Cover with wine, add herb bouquet, and cook in oven 15 minutes. Sauté the onions and mushrooms in the saucepan, adding more butter. Dredge lightly with flour, add cream, seasoning, and the wine poured off the fish. Cook 3 minutes, then pour into the casserole over the fish and bake 10 minutes in oven. Sprinkle with a little grated Parmesan cheese and a squeeze of lemon juice; put under broiler, brown very quickly, and serve in casserole.

TURBOT MORNAY AUX FINES HERBES

2 lbs. filets of turbot	2 sprigs parsley
2 Tbs. butter	1 tsp. lemon juice
¼ cup white wine	1 tsp. salt
½ cup water	¼ tsp. pepper
4 shallots (or 2 small	1 truffle
white onions)	Minced parsley
2 large mushrooms	Minced chives

Melt the butter in a pan and add the wine, water, parsley, lemon juice, salt and pepper. Place the fish in this and cover with buttered paper. Cook on top of the stove for 5 minutes, then 20 minutes in the oven. Take out fish and keep hot.

Put in the same pan the mushrooms and shallots chopped, with the rest of the butter, and cook for 5 minutes, stirring well. Add the truffle finely chopped, the minced parsley and chives, and shake the pan.

Make a sauce as follows:

Mornay Sauce

1 Tbs. melted butter	¼ tsp. cayenne pepper
1 Tbs. sifted flour	⅛ tsp. grated nutmeg
½ cup hot milk	4 Tbs. grated Parmesan cheese
½ tsp. salt	1 egg yolk

Heat butter in saucepan; add flour; stir well. Then add hot milk and seasoning and stir hard for 2 minutes. Add Parmesan cheese and cook 2 minutes, stirring well. Add egg yolk, mix briskly while cooking for 2 minutes without allowing to boil.

Cover the bottom of a baking-dish with about one-third of the prepared sauce. Place the fish on this and pour over the contents of the pan. Pour the rest of the sauce over the fish; add a little grated Parmesan cheese; set in oven for 15 minutes and serve in the same dish.

Filets of flounder or sole may be substituted for the turbot.

CHAPTER IV

MEATS AND POULTRY

LIST OF RECIPES

TONGUE
 Braised Tongue
 Beef Tongue (in paper cases)

CHICKEN
 Broiled Chicken (with Tarragon)
 Chicken Curry
 Chicken Fricassee (with Tarragon)
 Chicken Paprika
 Chicken Pilau
 Chicken (with Wine)

CHICKEN
 Chicken Hollandaise

DUCK
 Braised Duck
 Duck (with Tarragon)

GOOSE
 Jellied Goose

SQUAB
 Casserole of Squabs
 Squabs Florentine

If a soup can serve as the main dish of the meal, it is even easier for a meat stew to achieve that distinction. Indeed, it is sometimes difficult to distinguish between soups which have a tendency to thicken into stews and some stews which may be easily thinned into soups. Bouillabaisse may be either, but it is here listed under FISH. The herb bouquet goes into all of them and in different combinations according to the kind of meat and, it might be said, the nationality of the dish. The Italians favor onions, garlic, tomatoes, basil, rosemary (for lamb), and marjoram (for veal). The French, in addition to garlic, shallots, etc., use much tarragon, chervil, thyme, etc. Caraway seeds are popular in Hungary and Russia. In Latin countries, especially, there is one herb which runs like a *leitmotiv* through all their cookery, and if it is not allowed to become the main theme (as sometimes in Spain and Provence), it has almost a magic quality of transforming what might be mere dull food into a chef d'oeuvre of the cook's art. Garlic was the stand-by of the ancient Egyptians and later the Romans, who introduced it into all their provinces. The Anglo-Saxon alone seems to have shown resistance, but sometimes even an American or Britisher is trapped into eating dishes so subtly flavored by it that he does not suspect the presence of the dreaded garlic — and that is as it should be. And now garlic is recognized as a health food, put up in capsules and sold as a remedy for high blood pressure.

Rub a salad bowl with a clove of garlic, or a chicken about to be consigned to a casserole, or let it linger a few minutes in the butter or oil in which you are going to fry vegetables, or soup, or stew, and the magic has happened. It does taste better, but only the cook knows why.

Of the fine herbs, basil, fennel, and dill go well with fish and fish sauces. Marjoram is excellent with veal; rosemary with lamb or veal; tarragon with beef. The humble hamburger is delicious broiled with a sprinkling of mixed herbs; and sauces in endless variety, each flavored with a different combination of herbs, can transform and glorify the most inexpensive cuts of meat. It is interesting to experiment and work out new combinations, according to individual taste and the materials at hand. Anyone who does this will find cooking with herbs a real adventure.

RECIPES

BEEF

BRAISED BEEF OR DAUBE

3-lb. piece beef from rump
Sliced bacon
1 clove garlic
Nutmeg
¼ cup olive oil
Herb bouquet (celery, bay leaf, parsley)
1 small onion
1 sprig thyme
1 sprig marjoram
Lemon peel

1 cup stock and
1 cup boiling water (or 2 cups boiling water)
1 cup red wine
10 small white onions
New carrots, cooked
New potatoes, cooked
4 Tbs. butter
1 Tbs. flour
Salt
Pepper

Lard beef with strips of bacon; rub with garlic and dust with nutmeg; then marinate in the olive oil, with the onion, garlic, thyme, marjoram, lemon peel, salt and pepper.

Let stand for 2 hours, rubbing the oil into the beef from time to time.

Take meat out; dredge with flour and brown in butter on both sides in a deep casserole. Add herb bouquet and stock; cover and cook briskly for 10 minutes. Then add wine and let cook slowly in the oven for 3 hours, basting two or three times. Add small onions and cook 1 hour longer. Add the carrots and potatoes just before serving.

BEEF PAYSANNE

Left-over beef cut in small pieces	1 tsp. minced chives
2 medium white onions, cut up	1 tsp. minced chervil
2 Tbs. butter (or fat)	1 tsp. mustard
2 Tbs. flour	½ tsp. salt
1½ cups stock	¼ tsp. pepper
½ cup claret	1 Tbs. sherry

Cook onions in butter to a light brown, stirring constantly. Sprinkle in flour, stirring well. Add claret and stock and let boil 10 minutes. Add the beef, seasoning, herbs, and sherry. Mix well and cook about 20 minutes, stirring occasionally. Do not allow to boil after the meat is added.

BEEF STEW (MEXICAN)
(*with orégano*) [1]

1 lb. top round steak, cut in small pieces	1 tsp. chili sauce (or a little chili powder)
2 cups stock (or boiling water with bouillon cube)	1 tsp. orégano
1 large onion, minced	Salt (if bouillon cube is used less salt is needed)
½ green pepper, minced	Pepper
Bacon fat	
½ cup stewed tomatoes, fresh or canned (or 1 Tbs. tomato paste)	

Fry onion and pepper in bacon fat; add meat and brown well. Add the stock; season to taste and cook slowly in a covered pan, or transfer to a casserole in a slow oven. Add

[1] A dried wild marjoram found in Italian and Greek groceries; a dried herb from Mexico, a variety of sage.

tomatoes, orégano, and chili when nearly done. It should be cooked at least 2 hours or until meat is tender.

PLANKED HAMBURG STEAKS

1 lb. round of beef, ground with	1 tsp. minced chives
¼ lb. salt pork	1 tsp. minced parsley
Bacon	Salt
Mushrooms	Pepper
1 tsp. minced tarragon	

Form into round, flat cakes; surround each with a strip of bacon; fasten with toothpick; season and broil quickly on both sides. Then place on an oiled and heated plank and cook 5 minutes under broiler. Put on top of each meat cake a mushroom cap (which has been slightly browned in butter). Surround with a ring of mashed potatoes and small stuffed tomatoes. Sprinkle a pinch of mixed herbs on top of each meat cake and a little on the potatoes and tomatoes and serve on plank.

A few spoonfuls of cooked peas, string beans, or any other vegetables may be added before serving.

GRILLED STEAK MARCHAND DE VIN

2 T-bone steaks, 1¾ inch thick	1 tsp. beef extract (or bouillon cube), dissolved in
6 shallots (or 2 small white onions), chopped fine	1 tsp. boiling water (or 2 Tbs. rich stock)
½ cup red wine	Freshly ground pepper
4 Tbs. butter	Salt
2 tsp. lemon juice	1 clove garlic
1 Tbs. minced chervil	

Put shallots in an enamel pan with the wine. Reduce one half by boiling rapidly. Then add salt, pepper, and beef extract to the wine. In the meantime, cream butter, stirring in the lemon juice.

Now grill the steaks, being careful not to overcook them.

Place on a very hot platter. Add chervil to the butter and stir wine mixture in gradually. Pour over steaks; garnish with chervil and serve at once.

FILETS MIGNONS
(with mushroom sauce)

6 individual beef filets, cut 1¼-inch thick (about 1½ lbs.)	1 tsp. minced parsley
	1 tsp. lemon juice
6 large mushrooms	2 Tbs. butter
Salt	2 Tbs. sherry
Pepper	

Peel and sauté mushrooms in 1 Tbs. butter until brown. Add ½ tsp. salt, lemon juice, sherry, and parsley and keep hot while the filets are cooking. Shape the filets, holding them together with a toothpick; season and pan-broil in 1 Tbs. butter in very hot frying-pan 3 minutes on each side. Place on platter; arrange a mushroom on each; pour over sauce and serve.

Mushroom Sauce

4 mushrooms, peeled and chopped	4 sliced olives
2 minced shallots (or 1 tsp. minced white onion)	6 tarragon leaves, minced
	¼ tsp. salt
2 Tbs. butter	⅛ tsp. pepper
½ cup stock	½ cup white wine

Sauté onion in 1 Tbs. butter, sprinkle 1 tsp. flour; add mushrooms and cook 5 minutes. Add wine and reduce almost to a glacé, then add stock. Bring to a boil, add olives and seasonings; simmer 10 minutes and add tarragon. Take off fire and add 1 Tbs. butter, little by little.

HASH OF COLD BEEF

Left-over cooked beef	2 tsp. minced herbs
1 onion, sliced	(tarragon, parsley, chervil)
2 cups rich stock	¼ cup mushroom catsup
2 Tbs. butter	A few grains cayenne pepper
1 Tbs. flour (level)	A grating of nutmeg
	Salt

Melt butter in pan, add onion and herbs mixed together, and cook until they are a pale brown; then stir in flour and cook 3 minutes. Add seasoning and stock. Boil slowly for 10 minutes, then strain and add mushroom catsup. Add slices of beef and let them heat through without boiling. Serve with thin slices of toast. (Leyel.)

HUNGARIAN GOULASH

2 lbs. lean round beef (cut in 1½-inch cubes)	1 bay leaf
1 stalk celery	4 cloves
¼ lb. salt pork, minced	Parsley
1 large onion, minced	1 tsp. caraway seeds
½ green pepper, minced	1 clove garlic
2 cups tomatoes (or ½ cup tomato paste)	2 Tbs. paprika
	¾ tsp. salt
4 cups meat stock	2 Tbs. butter
	2 Tbs. flour

Brown the meat in fat thoroughly with minced onion. Add stock, green pepper, bay leaf, garlic, and other seasonings. Simmer for 2½ hours; then add thickening (butter, flour, and paprika creamed together). Add tomatoes and cook for a half hour longer. Serve with noodles.

MEAT CAKES

¾ lb. top round steak, ground with	1 tsp. minced parsley
¼ lb. salt pork	Salt
1 tsp. minced chives	Pepper
1 tsp. minced tarragon	Butter
1 tsp. minced marjoram	Flour

Form into cakes. Roll in flour seasoned with salt and pepper and fry in butter until well browned. Serve with a dab of butter and a sprig of fresh tarragon on each.

LAMB OR MUTTON

BROILED LAMB CHOPS
(*with dill*)

Broil loin chops, arrange on platter, season with salt and pepper, and put a dab of butter with ¼ tsp. minced dill on each one.

BROILED LAMB CHOPS
(*with tarragon*)

8 loin lamb chops	¼ tsp. salt
1 tsp. minced fresh tarragon	¼ tsp. pepper
(or ¼ tsp. dried)	2 Tbs. sherry
1 tsp. mustard	4 Tbs. cream
10 ripe olives, cut in half	

Trim off fat and grill the chops in a hot pan. When cooked, remove to a warming oven. Add to meat juices in the pan tarragon, butter, mustard, and seasoning. Blend thoroughly with drippings, then add wine. Reduce fire, and when all is blended add cream and olives. Simmer for 2 minutes, pour over chops, and serve.

DEVILLED CHOPS

English mutton chops, cut thick	A few drops onion juice
1 Tbs. butter	A few drops Chili sauce
1 tsp. French mustard	Juice of 1 lime
1 tsp. grated horseradish	Salt
1 tsp. hot chutney	Pepper
1 tsp. tarragon, minced	Cayenne pepper

Mix together butter, seasonings, and herbs. Rub this well into chops, broil rare, and put the rest of the sauce over them in a very hot dish.

LAMB CHOPS IN CASSEROLE

Lamb chops
Potatoes, cut to size of dollar
Onions, sliced
1 clove garlic
2 cups beef or veal stock

Herb bouquet (rosemary and parsley or thyme, bay leaf and parsley)
1 cup white wine
Salt
Pepper

Rub lamb with garlic, season, place in frying-pan with very hot fat and brown quickly on both sides. Cook onions in saucepan with butter (do not let them color). Place in a casserole a layer of potatoes, a layer of onions, and the chops. Place on top of this another layer of onions, the herbs, and then a layer of potatoes. Add wine, heavily seasoned stock, and a little thickening. Cover casserole and cook in oven 1½ hours. Remove cover and let the top brown a little before serving.

CURRY OF LAMB

2 lbs. shoulder or breast of lean lamb, cut in 1-inch squares
3 medium onions, chopped
1 clove garlic, chopped
1 green pepper, chopped
1 tart apple, chopped
1 stalk celery, chopped
2 bouillon cubes, dissolved in
4 cups hot water
1 bay leaf

1 sprig thyme
1 piece lemon rind
1 Tbs. lemon juice
4 Tbs. butter
2 Tbs. flour
2 Tbs. curry powder
¼ tsp. freshly ground pepper
2 tsp. salt
Milk from a fresh coconut

Melt the butter in a saucepan. Add the lamb and brown for a few minutes, stirring well. Dredge over flour; add curry and stir briskly for 3 minutes. Then add all the vegetables; cook for a few minutes, stirring well; add the stock, seasoning, bay leaf, thyme, and lemon rind and let simmer covered until well cooked, about 30 minutes. Add lemon juice and coconut milk and serve with rice, freshly grated coconut, and chutney.

CASSEROLE OF LAMB

1½ lbs. shoulder of lamb,
cut in pieces
1 onion, minced
1 small bunch new carrots
12 small white onions
12 small new potatoes
2 Tbs. butter (or fat)
3 cups boiling water

Herb bouquet (parsley, thyme,
and bay leaf, or rosemary and
parsley, or marjoram)
2 or **3** celery tops or leaves
6 peppercorns
½ tsp. salt
1 or **2** Tbs. flour, mixed with
cold water

Sauté the meat with minced onion in butter in frying-pan; when slightly browned, add boiling water and cook 5 minutes. Transfer to a casserole, add herb bouquet and seasonings; cover and cook in oven 1½ hours.

Meanwhile cook onions, carrots, and potatoes in boiling salted water. Add thickening to stew, then the cooked vegetables (after removing herb bouquet). Cover and cook a half hour longer. Stir well. Just before serving, a few cooked peas or string beans may be added.

LAMB PILAU

1 lb. lamb, cut in 2-inch pieces
3 onions, sliced
1 piece ginger root
1 bay leaf
6 peppercorns
1 saltspoon cardamom seeds
3 cups water

2 small onions
2 Tbs. seeded raisins
1 Tbs. almonds
1 cup rice
2 Tbs. butter
A little saffron
Salt

Boil lamb in water with onions, salt, and ginger root until tender. Remove lamb and simmer stock until reduced to sufficient quantity to cover rice. Brown meat in butter, add fried onions, raisins, almonds, cardamoms, bay leaf, rice, and peppercorns, and cover with stock. Boil until rice is tender, adding water if necessary. Color with a little saffron and put in oven until moisture evaporates and each grain of rice is separate from the others.

RAGOUT OF LAMB
(*with red wine*)

1½ lb. neck or shoulder of lamb, cut in 1-inch pieces
2 Tbs. olive oil
1 Tbs. salt
½ tsp. white pepper
2 cups white stock (or water)
1 cup tomato sauce
1 cup rich stock (or gravy)
½ cup claret
2 Tbs. flour
Rind of ½ lime or ¼ lemon

2 medium carrots
2 turnips
2 leeks
2 branches celery
2 sprigs parsley
1 sprig thyme
1 bay leaf
10 small white onions
2 medium-raw potatoes
2 or 3 Tbs. cooked green peas

Brown meat in oil briskly for 10 minutes with salt and pepper, stirring occasionally. Add flour, stir well, moisten with stock, tomato sauce, and wine. Mix well; cover the pan and boil for 10 minutes.

Scoop out carrots and turnips with small potato scoop and add them to the stew. Tie leeks, celery, parsley, thyme, and bay leaf in a bunch and place with the stew in a casserole; add lime; cover and cook in oven gently for 30 minutes. Peel onions and add to stew. Cook for 10 minutes longer. Scoop out potatoes with potato scoop and add to stew and cook again for 15 minutes. Remove herbs; stir well and add peas. Serve in the casserole.

ROAST LEG OF LAMB
(*with rosemary*)

Leg of lamb
1 clove garlic
Olive oil

1 sprig rosemary
(or 1 tsp. dried)
Salt

Rub lamb with garlic. Cut a slit and place in it the rosemary. Sew up slit, add salt, and place in oven, basting occasionally with olive oil.

LAMB PAPRIKA

1 lb. mutton	½ cup tomatoes
1 medium onion	½ cup stock
4 strips bacon	½ cup red wine
Butter	Caraway seeds
Potatoes	1 sprig rosemary
1 Tbs. paprika	Salt
1 Tbs. flour	Pepper

Cut up onion and fry in butter. Add mutton, cut into small pieces dredged with flour, the bacon, and potatoes peeled and cut in slices. Fry all a pale brown. Put potatoes, meat and onion, and rosemary into a casserole and cook slowly a half hour. Add paprika, seasoning, wine, tomatoes, stock, and caraway seeds (in a muslin bag). Cook a half hour longer and serve in casserole.

LAMB STEAKS BROILED
(*with fine herbs*)

3 lamb steaks, cut 1 inch thick (from top of leg of lamb)	1 tsp. minced parsley
	2 tsp. lemon juice
6 shallots (or 3 small white onions)	½ cup claret
	3 Tbs. butter
1 bouillon cube, dissolved in	Salt
1 tsp. boiling water	Pepper
1 tsp. minced rosemary	

Mince the shallots and put them with the claret into an enamel saucepan. Reduce one half by boiling rapidly. Add freshly ground pepper and the bouillon. Cream the butter and stir into it the lemon juice. Now rub the steaks with garlic and a little olive oil, sprinkle with a little salt, and broil, being careful not to overcook them. Place them on a very hot platter. Add the rosemary and parsley to the butter and stir the wine in gradually. Pour over the steaks, garnish with parsley, and serve at once.

VEAL

CASSEROLE OF VEAL
(with marjoram)

1 lb. breast of veal, cut up	4 peppercorns
1 medium onion, minced	½ tsp. salt
8 small onions	Sweet marjoram
8 small carrots	Parsley
8 small potatoes	2½ cups boiling water

Sauté veal in fat with onion. Add boiling water and cook for a few minutes, stirring well. Transfer to casserole, add herbs and seasoning, and cook about 2½ hours in oven.

Meanwhile cook onions, carrots, and potatoes in boiling salted water. Add a little thickening to the stew (1 Tbs. flour, mixed well with cold water), then add cooked vegetables, cover, and cook a half hour longer. Just before serving, a few young peas or string beans (cooked) may be added.

ITALIAN VEAL ROLLS

Veal cutlet, cut into 6 individual portions (4-inch square)	½ tsp. minced rosemary
	½ tsp. minced sage (half the amount if dried)
6 thin slices boiled ham	1 Tbs. butter
6 sausages	Salt
¼ cup olive oil	Pepper

Pound the veal slices until flattened but not too thin. Place over each a slice of ham; sprinkle with the herbs mixed together, dotting each with ½ tsp. butter, and then roll each one around a sausage. Skewer to keep the roll secure and place in baking-dish with the olive oil. Add seasoning and bake in moderate oven (350°) about one hour. Serve in the same dish.

LEFT-OVER VEAL
(with tarragon)

Slices of left-over	1 cup stock
cooked veal	1 Tbs. minced tarragon
1 Tbs. butter	Salt
1 Tbs. flour	Pepper

Cook the butter and flour together in a saucepan, add the stock, and stir well. Add seasoning and the tarragon, then add pieces of veal and allow to heat without boiling.

RACK OF VEAL, BRETONNE

3 lbs. rack of veal	1 tsp. minced marjoram
2 Tbs. melted butter	1 tsp. minced thyme
2 Tbs. cold water	1 tsp. salt
1 clove garlic	½ tsp. pepper

Trim the veal; rub with garlic and place in a small roasting-pan. Season with salt and pepper and the herbs. Spread the melted butter over the veal and pour the cold water into the pan. Set in oven and roast three-quarters of an hour, turning once in a while and basting frequently with own gravy. Place on serving platter, skim off the gravy, and then pour over the meat. Serve with beans Bretonne (see page 107) on the same platter.

RAGOUT NO. 1

2 lbs. veal, cut into individual cutlets	Herb bouquet (1 bay leaf, 1 sprig parsley, 1 sprig thyme)
¼ lb. fat bacon, sliced	2 Tbs. butter
2 large onions, cut in rings	1 tsp. vinegar
½ cup milk	Salt
¼ cup sour cream	Pepper

Put the butter in a casserole with a well-fitting lid. Stir until melted. Lay the slices of bacon side by side so that they cover bottom of casserole. On this lay the onion rings and the herb bouquet. Leave the pan uncovered on the fire and sprinkle both sides of the cutlets with salt and pepper. When the bacon and onions are hot lay in the veal, put on the lid, and let it stew gently for 1½ hours. Take out veal and bacon, remove herb bouquet, and arrange on hot serving-dish. Sprinkle a little flour in the pan, pour in the milk, with the vinegar and sour cream, and put back on the fire. Stir until the gravy thickens into a brown sauce. Pour over the veal and serve with boiled rice.

RAGOUT NO. 2
(with mushrooms)

1½ lbs. veal cutlet	Lemon juice
¼ lb. mushrooms	2 Tbs. butter
Bouquet mixed herbs	Salt
1 cup stock	Flour
2 Tbs. cream	1 egg yolk
1 clove garlic	

Fry the veal in butter. Make a sauce with the mushrooms, cut in shreds, the mixed herbs, garlic, and the butter, and dredge in a little flour. Put all these ingredients in a saucepan, add stock, and let it reduce. Put veal in sauce; add lemon juice and the yolk of an egg mixed with a little cream.

ROAST OF VEAL LOIN
(with rosemary)

Loin or shoulder of veal	1 clove garlic
2 Tbs. olive oil	½ tsp. freshly ground pepper
2 Tbs. cold water	1 tsp. salt
2 or 3 sprigs rosemary	

Rub veal with garlic, then cut two or three slits in meat and insert a sprig of rosemary in each one (if dried rosemary is used, sew up slit). Add seasoning, pour oil over the meat and water in the bottom of pan. Baste well and serve with the pan gravy.

SCALOPPINI PARMIGIANO

1 lb. veal cutlet, sliced thin	2 or 3 sprigs sweet marjoram
2 Tbs. olive oil	⅛ tsp. nutmeg
1 cup veal or beef stock	1 Tbs. lemon juice
⅓ cup Marsala (or sherry)	Salt
1 Tbs. flour	Pepper
1 Tbs. butter	Parmesan cheese

Cut the veal into pieces 3 in. square. Pound well, dredge with grated Parmesan cheese, and brown slowly in olive oil. Add stock and wine. Season to taste, add nutmeg and marjoram; cover and simmer until very tender. Thicken gravy with flour and butter cooked together; sprinkle with lemon juice and serve at once.

SAVORY CUTLETS

1½ lbs. veal, cut into individual servings	½ cup stock
	½ cup white wine
1½ Tbs. mixed fine herbs, minced	2 Tbs. butter
1 tsp. celery, minced	1 egg
1 tsp. onion, minced	½ tsp. salt
¾ cup fine bread crumbs	Pepper

Dip pieces of veal in the slightly beaten egg, then in the bread crumbs, which have been mixed with the herbs. Melt butter in a saucepan, cook onion and celery 3 minutes. Brown the veal in this on both sides and remove to a casserole. Add wine and stock to saucepan, with seasoning, boil up once and pour over the veal. Cover and bake about 40 minutes or until done. Serve in casserole.

VEAL PAPRIKA

2½ lbs. breast of veal	Pepper
2 Tbs. fat	1 Tbs. flour
1 large onion, cut fine	Parsley
1 Tbs. paprika	Caraway seeds
Salt	½ cup sour cream

Sauté onion slowly in fat in a heavy frying-pan until a

light yellow. Cut veal into 1 in. cubes, add to the onion, and dredge with flour. Cover and allow to steam together for a few minutes; stir well, then sprinkle with salt and pepper to taste and the paprika. Add enough warm water to cover the meat and cook covered slowly for 1½ hours. Just before serving add the sour cream. Allow to cook up well and serve in a border of mashed potatoes or rice.

PORK

LOIN OF PORK AND BEANS

3 lbs. loin of pork	1 sprig rosemary
1 clove garlic	1 tsp. salt
1 Tbs. butter (or fat)	½ tsp. pepper
½ cup cold water	1 lb. cooked white beans

Place pork in a roasting-pan. Sprinkle over salt and pepper. Make an incision with a knife in the middle of the loin about 1½ in. deep. Insert garlic and rosemary, then spread butter over meat. Add water and roast in a hot oven for 1 hour, taking care to turn it every 10 minutes, and to baste frequently with own gravy. Remove roast to a hot platter. Skim fat off gravy, then add to pan the cooked and well-drained beans; briskly toss them. Place roasting-pan on the fire and boil 2 minutes. Arrange beans around loin and serve.

To cook white beans:

2 cups navy beans	2 sprigs parsley
2 qts. cold water	2 oz. piece salt pork
1 medium carrot, cut in quarters	1 clove garlic
2 leeks	1 tsp. salt
1 medium onion, cut in half	½ tsp. pepper

Soak beans in cold water for 12 hours. Drain well and put them in a saucepan with 2 qts. cold water and the vegetables tied together. Add pork, garlic, and seasoning. Cover the pan and let simmer on a slow fire for 1½ hours.

Take out vegetables, herbs, and pork; drain the beans. Chop the pork and mix with the beans.

STUFFED PORK CHOPS

6 chops cut thick and slit on side	1 cup water or stock
	3 cups savory stuffing

Fill the incisions with the stuffing and fasten with small skewers. Arrange the chops in a baking-dish, add about 1 cup of water or stock, cover, and bake in a moderate oven for a half hour; uncover and bake three-quarters of an hour longer or until tender, basting frequently. Add more water if necessary and serve in casserole.

Savory Stuffing

3 cups toasted bread crumbs	1 tsp. sweet marjoram, minced fresh
1 large onion, minced	1 tsp. thyme or sage, minced fresh
1 tsp. grated lemon peel	1 tsp. celery leaves, minced fresh
2 tsp. salt	1 tsp. parsley, minced fresh (if dried
2 Tbs. butter	herbs are used, half the quantity)
¼ tsp. pepper	1 egg
1 tsp. summer savory, minced fresh	

Mix herbs, seasonings, and crumbs. Fry onion in butter until golden brown and mix with the other ingredients. Stir in the egg slightly beaten, and if too dry add about ½ cup hot water.

NO. 1 SAUSAGE MEAT

2 lbs. fresh lean pork	2 Tbs. fresh basil
1 lb. fat pork	1 Tbs. fresh marjoram, chopped
1 clove garlic	1 Tbs. fresh thyme, chopped
Salt	(half the amount if dried)
Pepper	

Put the pork through meat grinder and work the fat and the lean together until well blended. Add herbs, salt and pepper to taste. Work well with the hands or with a wooden spoon until thoroughly mixed. Pack in a deep pan and keep on ice until needed.

NO. 2 CREOLE

2 lbs. lean pork	½ tsp. cayenne pepper
1 lb. fat pork	1½ tsp. salt
1 large onion, minced	1 tsp. black pepper
1 clove garlic, minced	1 tsp. minced thyme
½ tsp. chili pepper	2 tsp. minced parsley
½ tsp. red pepper	1 bay leaf
(paprika or pimento)	¼ tsp. allspice

Chop pork very fine and mix together. Season; then add red pepper, minced onion and garlic, and the herbs, then the spices, mixed thoroughly. Work over and over till thoroughly mixed; then keep cool and make into sausages or flat cakes and fry in lard. Serve with lentil purée (p. 110).

CREOLE JAMBALAYA

1½ cups rice	2 sprigs parsley
1 lb. fresh pork	1 bay leaf
12 pork sausages	⅛ tsp. ground cloves
1 slice ham	2 qts. beef stock
2 medium-sized onions	½ tsp. chili pepper
1 Tbs. butter	Salt
2 cloves garlic	Pepper
2 sprigs thyme	Cayenne

Chop pork fine, mince onions, brown them in butter slowly, stirring constantly. Add ham and garlic and cook 3 minutes; then the minced herbs, spice, and bay leaf and let brown 5 minutes; then add sausages whole and cook 5 minutes longer. Add stock, let come to a boil, and add rice which has been carefully washed, and the seasoning. Boil a half hour or until rice is cooked.

HAM BAKED IN CIDER

1 ham	1 cup brown sugar
1 qt. sweet cider	Cloves and brown sugar

Soak ham overnight. Barely cover ham with water, add sugar and cider (if cider is very sweet, use less sugar). Boil 3 hours or until skin will peel off easily. Remove skin, cover the ham with a crust of brown sugar; stick with cloves, and bake in a slow oven for 3 hours. Baste frequently with liquor in which ham was boiled and pour around ham on platter. Serve with cider applesauce.

SAVORY BAKED HAM

2 lbs. mild ham, sliced ¾ in. thick	1 Tbs. minced parsley
4 Tbs. brown sugar	1 sprig fresh rosemary
1 tsp. dry mustard	(or 1 tsp. dried)
¾ cup dry white or red wine, or 1 cup cider	

Parboil ham to remove salt, then rub into both sides the mustard and sugar mixed. Lay the slices in shallow baking-dish, pour over a little water and the wine or cider. Cover and bake slowly 1 hour, basting frequently. Serve with sweet potatoes and applesauce or compote.

KIDNEYS

LAMB KIDNEYS
(*with fine herbs*)

8 lamb kidneys	Herb bouquet
½ cup mushrooms	1 tsp. lemon juice
2 Tbs. butter	½ cup Madeira, sherry, or
1 Tbs. flour	white wine
1 Tbs. bouillon	Salt
	Pepper

Peel kidneys and cut in slices. Sauté in butter with mushrooms cut into pieces. Remove from butter; add flour, bouillon, herb bouquet, and seasoning. Cook 15 minutes gently. Then put back the kidneys, add wine and lemon juice, and reheat for 5 minutes.

LAMB KIDNEYS
(*with red wine*)

8 lamb kidneys	½ cup red wine
2 shallots, chopped	1 small piece celery
1 slice garlic	Small bouquet parsley
1 carrot	1 pinch thyme
3 Tbs. butter	Salt
1 Tbs. flour	Pepper
1 cup stock	

Split the kidneys lengthwise and remove all fibers and skin. Soak in cold water for 1 hour, changing the water several times. Heat the butter in a saucepan, add shallots, garlic, and carrot, and brown slightly. Add flour and brown a little more, then pour in stock and wine. Add remaining seasonings, and when boiling put in the kidneys, which have been well drained. Cook until kidneys are tender. Place the kidneys on a small hot dish and strain the sauce over them. Serve on triangles of toast fried in butter.

VEAL KIDNEYS
(*with wine*)

3 veal kidneys	1 bay leaf
1 onion, minced	Minced parsley
1 clove garlic	Cayenne pepper
6 mushrooms, minced	1 Tbs. butter
2 Tbs. butter	1 Tbs. flour
½ cup stock	1 Tbs. sherry
½ cup white wine	Salt

Wash kidneys well; remove fat and sinewy parts and split them in half. Sauté onion in butter, cook to a light

brown. Then add the kidneys; season and cook 5 minutes, turning frequently.

Lift kidneys out with a skimmer and keep hot. Sauté the mushrooms 5 minutes, then add stock, wine, garlic, and bay leaf. Cook 10 minutes. Combine butter and flour and add little by little to the sauce. Cook 3 minutes; then add the kidneys with the parsley, cayenne pepper, and sherry. Cook 2 minutes and serve on thin slices of toast.

LIVER

BRAISED CALVES' LIVER

1 whole liver	1 bay leaf
Fat salt pork	1 sprig thyme
¼ cup diced carrot	1 sprig parsley
¼ cup diced onion	2 cloves
¼ cup diced celery	4 peppercorns
2 cups stock (or water)	1 Tbs. butter
1 cup white wine	1 Tbs. flour

Prepare liver, skewer and tie in shape. Lard upper side with strips of salt pork. Put in deep pan with trimmings from the pork, carrot, onion, celery, cloves, peppercorns, herbs, stock, and wine. Cover closely and bake 2 hours in slow oven (300° F.), uncovering the last 20 minutes. Remove from pan, strain liquor, and thicken with butter and flour, browned together. Serve around liver.

CALVES' LIVER
(with red wine)

1½ lbs. calves' liver, sliced ¾ in. thick	1 tsp. minced parsley
2 Tbs. butter	1 tsp. minced chives
1 Tbs. flour	1 tsp. minced celery
6 mushrooms, sliced	1 sprig thyme, minced
¾ cup red wine	Salt
	Pepper

Cut the liver into individual servings. Heat in butter,

turning two or three times. Add the herbs, seasoning, and wine; simmer 3 to 5 minutes. Take out liver and keep hot. Add the mushrooms to sauce, boil up, and cook 3 minutes. Thicken with flour and 1 Tbs. butter cooked together, and pour over the liver.

CALVES' LIVER
(with fine herbs)

Slices of liver, cut ¾ in. thick	Chives, chopped
3 Tbs. butter	Chervil, chopped
1 Tbs. flour	1 tsp. lemon juice
¼ cup white wine	Salt
Parsley, chopped	Pepper

Cook liver in 2 Tbs. butter over a good heat until the blood comes out. Keep liver hot, and add wine, thicken with butter and flour cooked together, stir sediment in pan to thicken and color gravy. Add 1 Tbs. butter, lemon juice, and chopped herbs. Pour gravy over liver and serve.

CHICKEN LIVERS
(with mushrooms)

6 chicken livers	1 tsp. minced chives
¼ lb. mushrooms	2 Tbs. sherry
2 Tbs. butter	Salt
1 tsp. minced chervil	Flour

Peel and slice mushrooms. Sauté them in 1 Tbs. butter; then add the rest of the butter and the livers and cook about 3 minutes, turning over several times. Sprinkle with a little flour, stir well, and add the sherry. Cook 3 minutes longer, then add the herbs and serve on thin triangles of toast.

TONGUE

BRAISED TONGUE

1 fresh beef tongue	½ cup white or red **wine**
⅓ cup diced carrots	1 sprig parsley
⅓ cup diced onions	1 sprig thyme
⅓ cup diced celery	1 sprig marjoram
½ cup white wine	1 bay leaf

Wipe tongue and put in kettle, cover with boiling water, and let simmer 2 hours. Take tongue from water, remove skin and roots. Place in deep baking-pan and surround with the vegetables and herbs. Pour over 4 cups of the sauce and the wine; cover closely and bake two hours, turning after the first hour. Put on platter and strain sauce around it.

Sauce

¼ cup butter	2 tsp. salt
¼ cup flour	½ tsp. pepper
2½ cups liquor (in which tongue was cooked)	1½ cups tomatoes, stewed and strained
1 tsp. Worcestershire sauce	

Melt the butter and stir until brown. Add the flour, cooking until well browned. Then pour in gradually, stirring constantly, liquor from the tongue. Bring to boiling point and add tomatoes. Bring again to the boiling point; add Worcestershire sauce and seasoning.

BEEF TONGUE
(*in paper cases*)

6 slices tongue	1 tsp. chervil, minced
6 slices bacon	1 tsp. minced parsley
6 anchovies	1 tsp. minced tarragon
3 shallots	3 capers

Cover each slice of tongue with a mixture of the herbs

and capers; add a mashed anchovy. Roll each slice of tongue as you would a jelly roll with a slice of bacon on the outside. Wrap in a piece of cooking-paper, folding it tightly so that the juices will not escape. Cook in a very hot oven (500° F.) for 10 minutes. Remove paper and serve at once.

CHICKEN

BROILED CHICKEN
(*with tarragon*)

Split the chicken and rub with garlic, then brown quickly on both sides under a very hot broiler. Place in dripping-pan in oven and baste with hot water and butter until done. Just before taking out of oven, season and sprinkle with finely minced tarragon and serve with pan gravy.

CHICKEN CURRY

2 chickens (fryers)	½ tsp. ginger
6 cups water	1 Tbs. Worcestershire sauce
3 medium onions, minced	⅛ tsp. Tabasco sauce
2 apples, minced	1 fresh coconut
6 stalks celery, minced	4 Tbs. flour
½ cup olive oil	2 cups heavy cream
1 tsp. salt	2 egg yolks, well beaten
4 Tbs. curry powder	6 cups boiled rice
¼ tsp. pepper	

Wash chickens and cut into pieces. Cook in water until tender. Cook onions, apples, and celery in olive oil until slightly browned. Add curry powder and simmer 5 minutes longer. Add 4 cups stock from the chicken and remaining seasonings. Cook 20 minutes. Blend in flour and cook until mixture thickens, stirring constantly.

Cut chicken into smaller pieces, removing bones. Add to thickened mixture with milk drained from the coconut. Allow to stand for 3 hours. When ready to serve, add cream and beaten egg yolks. Heat thoroughly and serve at once over hot rice.

Pass grated coconut, chutney, and chopped peanuts.

CHICKEN FRICASSEE
(*with tarragon*)

1 fricasseeing chicken, cut up
2 cups water (or chicken stock)
4 Tbs. butter
4 Tbs. flour
Several small white onions
1 Tbs. minced tarragon or minced dill

1 egg yolk
2 sprigs tarragon
1 clove garlic
1 tsp. salt
Boiled rice

Rub pieces of chicken with garlic and dredge in flour. Brown in butter. Blend 2 Tbs. butter with 2 Tbs. flour and make a sauce with 2 cups water. Lay chicken in deep skillet, pour the sauce over it. Add onions and salt. Cook until chicken is tender; add hot water to have about 2 cups liquid for gravy. Remove chicken to hot platter.

Make gravy by heating 3 Tbs. of the liquid from the kettle with the egg yolk and stir back into the remaining liquid. Add chopped tarragon and boil 5 minutes. One teaspoonful fresh dill may be used instead of tarragon.

Pile on a hot platter the boiled rice and arrange chicken around it. Serve extra gravy in a bowl.

CHICKEN PAPRIKA

4-lb. fowl or 2 fryers
2 large, mild onions, minced
5 Tbs. fat
1 Tbs. paprika

1 tsp. salt
2 cups water
1 cup sour cream

Sauté onions in fat until brown. Stir in paprika and simmer 3 or 4 minutes. Wash and dry fowl. Disjoint and cut into pieces for serving. Dust with salt, add to first mixture with water and simmer covered until tender. Just before serving remove pan from heat, cool slightly, then stir in the sour cream.

CHICKEN PILAU

⅓ cup cold chicken, cut up	⅔ cup canned or stewed
1½ cups rice, boiled	fresh tomatoes
3 Tbs. butter	½ cup chicken stock

Melt butter in saucepan; add the boiled rice and cook 3 minutes. Add tomatoes, chicken, and stock. Cook 5 minutes and season with salt and a little cayenne. One teaspoon minced basil or 2 tsp. tarragon may be sprinkled over the top just before serving.

Cold lamb may be substituted for chicken.

CHICKEN
(with wine)

3 lbs. frying chicken	1 cup sour cream
1 clove garlic	Salt
4 Tbs. butter	Pepper
2 cups Sauterne	

Cut up chicken and rub with garlic. Brown in butter. Add wine and simmer chicken on top of range until tender, basting frequently. Just before serving add sour cream and stir well. Season to taste. Serve with rice.

CHICKEN HOLLANDAISE

1 chicken, cut into 8 pieces	3 egg yolks
2 onions, cut up	1 lemon
2 Tbs. butter	Salt
1 Tbs. flour	Pepper
Herb bouquet or tarragon	

Cover fowl with water and boil it for three-quarters of an

hour with the onions, herbs, and salt. Melt butter in a saucepan, stir in flour, and make a sauce with some of the water chicken has boiled in. Simmer 10 minutes.

Beat up egg yolks, add juice of lemon and 1 tsp. minced tarragon. Stir into sauce very slowly till it has consistency of cream. If necessary add a little more salt and pepper. Arrange pieces of chicken on dish it is to be served in. Pour over sauce and serve.

DUCK

BRAISED DUCK

1 duck, cut up as if for fricasseeing	2 sprigs parsley, minced
2 oz. salt pork, cut up	1 sprig thyme, minced (or 1 saltspoon, powdered)
1 small carrot, sliced	1 bay leaf
1 onion, sliced	2 cloves
1 leek, sliced	10 peppercorns
6 Tbs. butter	½ lb. mushrooms
1 Tbs. flour	Salt
½ clove garlic, crushed	Pepper

Brown pieces of duck in butter in frying-pan. Make a stock of the neck, wings and cut-up giblets. Add this stock with seasoning to duck and let simmer 20 minutes.

Meanwhile arrange the salt pork, vegetables, herbs, and spices in a casserole. Lay the pieces of duck on the top of these and pour over stock. Cover and bake in oven 1 hour or until duck is tender.

Sauté mushrooms in butter, dredge with flour, and add some of stock from the duck, cooking into a thick gravy. Add this to duck in the casserole, stirring in well; reheat and serve in casserole. Serve with brown or wild rice.

DUCK
(*with tarragon*)

5-lb. duck	3 sprigs fresh tarragon
2 oz. salt pork	2 Tbs. melted butter
1 small carrot, sliced	2 Tbs. flour
1 onion, sliced	2 tsp. salt
1 leek, sliced	1 tsp. white pepper
1 cup beef stock	½ cup claret
½ cup tomatoes, stewed	10 mushrooms, sliced and
and strained	sautéed in butter

Clean and wipe inside of duck. Singe and truss. Arrange salt pork and vegetables in a large baking-pan. Lay duck over this. Season and add butter. Place on a brisk fire and cook 15 minutes, turning over once in a while. Add flour to vegetables in pan; stir well with a spoon, pour in wine, stock, and tomato sauce. Mix well and again cover the pan and cook 10 minutes.

Pick off the leaves of tarragon, put them aside and add stalks to the duck. Place in hot oven for three-quarters of an hour, turning the duck once in a while. Remove, untruss, place on a hot dish and keep warm.

Place pan on the fire, skim the fat surface off the sauce, and boil 8 minutes. Strain the sauce through a sieve into a saucepan. Add the tarragon leaves and mushrooms, then let the sauce reduce to ½ pt., mixing occasionally meanwhile. Pour the sauce over duck and serve.

GOOSE

JELLIED GOOSE

1 goose	2 Tbs. gelatine to each
2 large onions, sliced	pint of stock
1 Tbs. savory mixed herbs,	Hard-boiled eggs, sliced
or herb bouquet: 1 sprig	Salt
thyme, celery, bay leaf	Pepper

Stew the goose until quite tender in water that just

covers it, with the seasoning, onions, and herbs. When done, remove the meat from the bones; return the latter to saucepan and cook for another 15 minutes. Skim off the fat, strain the liquid through muslin. Mix soaked gelatine in stock.

Set a little of the liquid at the bottom of a mold, arrange eggs on it, and cover with more stock. Let this set, then fill up with the goose meat cut in even-sized pieces and pour the stock over all of it. Turn out when set and serve with cold applesauce.

SQUAB

CASSEROLE OF SQUABS

6 squabs	Herb bouquet:
6 tsp. butter or fat	2 sprigs parsley
1 onion, finely minced	1 sprig chervil
1 green pepper, minced	1 sprig thyme
1 oz. raw lean ham	1 bay leaf
1 cup rich stock	1 clove
1 Tbs. butter	1 tsp. salt
1 clove garlic	½ tsp. pepper
	1 cup cooked green peas

Place the squabs in a pan, spread 1 tsp. butter over each one, and set in a brisk oven for 15 minutes or until nicely browned all over.

Meanwhile put onion, pepper, and ham in an earthen casserole with 1 Tbs. butter and fry for 5 minutes, lightly stirring. Add the squabs to this and the seasoning, stock, herb bouquet, garlic, and clove. Mix lightly; cover and set in oven for 1 hour. Remove, take out herb bouquet. Add cooked peas and serve in the casserole.

SQUABS FLORENTINE

The above recipe may be varied by omitting the peas and adding a few small broiled sausages and about a dozen boiled chestnuts which have been slightly sautéed in butter.

CHAPTER V

SAUCES

'Sixty religions and only one sauce,' said Voltaire of England in the eighteenth century.

'On devient cuisinier, on est né saucier,' was said by another Frenchman.

Herbs are indispensable in the making of meat and fish sauces, and the variety of combinations is endless. Our cookery, like that of the English in Voltaire's time, is sadly lacking both in the variety and quality of its sauces. Their preparation requires a certain knack as well as great care, and they should be served as soon as made. Perhaps this explains their lack of popularity in this era of quick lunches and mass-production cookery.

RECIPES

SAUCE À L'ARNOUX

¼ lb. butter	1 bay leaf
1 onion, minced	2 cloves
1 small carrot, minced	A sprig of thyme
3 Tbs. flour	4 white peppercorns
2 cups bouillon	½ tsp. salt
1 cup red wine	

Melt butter and brown onion and carrot. Add flour, mixing well until smooth and browning well. Add the meat juice you have saved and enough water to make the required amount of liquid. Use a bouillon cube if there is not enough meat juice to give a good flavor. Add seasonings and stir continuously until the sauce comes to a boil. Let cook 20 minutes, add wine, and strain. Add the sliced or diced cold meat and heat thoroughly. Serve with a mold of rice, or with plain boiled potatoes sprinkled with parsley.

For lamb gravy, add a clove of garlic if roast is not stuck with garlic in the first place. Try a pinch of sweet marjoram with the thyme, as marjoram is good with lamb.

For veal, instead of thyme and marjoram use ½ tsp. rosemary.

SAUCE BÉARNAISE

3 Tbs. tarragon vinegar	Bouquet of tarragon leaves
1 Tbs. cold water	6 peppercorns
1 Tbs. minced shallots	½ bay leaf
¼ lb. butter	½ tsp. salt
4 egg yolks, slightly beaten	1 tsp. minced tarragon

Cook the vinegar, shallots, peppercorns, and herbs together until liquid is reduced by half. Strain, add cold water, and pour gradually over egg yolks in double boiler, stirring well. Divide the butter into six portions; add one at a time, stirring over hot water. Stir continuously until the sauce is smooth as thick cream. At the last add salt and the minced tarragon.

CHEESE SAUCE ('MORNAY')

2 Tbs. melted butter	4 Tbs. grated Parmesan cheese
2 Tbs. sifted flour	or ⅓ cup strong American
1 cup hot milk	⅛ tsp. cayenne pepper
¼ tsp. onion juice	⅛ tsp. grated nutmeg
½ tsp. salt	

Heat butter in saucepan, add flour, stir well, and cook 5 minutes. Add hot milk and seasoning and stir hard for 2 minutes. Add the cheese and cook 2 minutes, stirring well.

CHERVIL SAUCE
(for broiled fish)

¼ lb. butter
1 Tbs. chervil, minced fine

Heat together and pour over the fish. A few blanched almonds added to this sauce is very good. This same drawn-butter sauce with tarragon or basil may be used for broiled fish.

CURRY SAUCE

2 cups stock	¼ tsp. ginger
(chicken, lamb, or veal)	½ tsp. salt
2 medium onions, minced	⅛ tsp. pepper
1 clove garlic	1 Tbs. flour
¼ cup olive oil	1 tsp. Worcestershire sauce
1 tart apple, minced	¼ tsp. Tabasco sauce
3 stalks celery, minced	(Optional: milk from coconut,
1 bay leaf	egg yolk, and cream)
2 Tbs. curry	

Cook onions, garlic, apple, celery, and bay leaf in oil until slightly browned. Remove garlic and add curry mixed with flour; simmer 5 minutes, stirring well; then add stock and rest of ingredients. Cook 20 minutes, stirring occasionally. The milk of a coconut may be added just before serving and 1 or 2 egg yolks mixed with ½ cup cream.

A Recipe for Curry Powder

1 oz. ginger	¼ oz. cayenne pepper
1 oz. coriander seed	3 oz. turmeric
1 oz. cardamom seed	1 oz. cumin seed

Have the ingredients finely powdered and put up in separate papers. Mix well in a dry warm place, then put the mixture in a jar or wide-mouthed bottle. Seal and keep in a dry place.

DILL SAUCE

1 Tbs. chopped dill, added to a sauce made with stock thickened with a little flour browned in butter, or added to a plain-butter sauce, or mixed with plain mayonnaise.

HOT DILL SAUCE, SWEDISH

Strain off some of the broth when making lamb stew; thicken with a little flour and butter; add some cream and a few drops of vinegar and chopped fresh dill.

DRAWN BUTTER SAUCE

4 Tbs. butter	1 Tbs. minced herbs
2 Tbs. flour	(basil, chervil, and
1½ cups hot fish stock (water	chives, or dill and
in which fish was cooked)	parsley, or fennel
½ tsp. salt	and parsley, or
⅛ tsp. pepper	minced tarragon)
1 tsp. lemon juice	

Melt half the butter, add flour and seasoning. Cook well.

Pour stock on gradually and boil 5 minutes. Add remaining butter in small bits and then the minced herbs. Serve with fish.

FENNEL SAUCE

1 Tbs. chopped fennel, added to a sauce made with fish or meat stock, thickened with a little flour browned in butter, or added to a plain butter sauce, or mixed with plain mayonnaise.

GARLIC SAUCE ('AYOLI')

2 cups olive oil	Soft bread crumb
3 cloves garlic	(about size of an egg)
2 yolks of hard-boiled eggs	1 tsp. lemon juice
	1 saltspoon salt

Peel the garlic and put it in a mortar and mash to a paste. Add the bread crumbs, which have been soaked in lukewarm water and pressed out. Add the egg yolks and salt. Add the oil to the paste drop by drop as if making mayonnaise, adding from time to time a few drops of lemon juice. When oil is all absorbed the sauce should be smooth and compact. Add a few drops of cold water at the end. (An important point to remember is that the oil must be neither hot nor cold.)

GREEN MAYONNAISE ('RAVIGOTE')

Tarragon	Watercress
Parsley	2 or 3 chives
Chervil	1 leaf lettuce (or spinach)
Few drops lemon juice	

Take a few sprigs of the herbs and a leaf of lettuce or spinach and pound them in a mortar with some drops of lemon juice. Squeeze out the juice of the herbs, and mix it with mayonnaise sauce. A few green peas will add to the color and consistency of sauce.

HERB BUTTER SAUCES

The basic recipe is the same for all and may be varied almost indefinitely, according to the number and variety of herbs available as well as the variety of fish for which they are used.

¼ cup butter	1½ Tbs. minced herbs
½ tsp. salt	(basil, chervil, and
⅛ tsp. pepper	chives, or dill and
½ Tbs. lemon juice	parsley, or fennel
	and parsley, or tar-
	ragon)

Work butter with small wooden spoon until creamy. Add ingredients and work them in with a spoon; last of all the lemon juice drop by drop.

HORSERADISH SAUCE NO. 1

1 cup grated fresh horseradish	1 Tbs. vinegar
½ tsp. salt	1 cup whipped cream
¼ tsp. mustard	

Mix horseradish, salt, mustard, and vinegar. Let stand a half hour, then add the whipped cream and serve. (From an old English recipe.)

HORSERADISH SAUCE NO. 2

1 cup sour cream	¼ cup prepared horseradish
¼ tsp. salt	2 Tbs. minced parsley
Dash of pepper	

Blend ingredients in order given. Chill thoroughly and serve as relish with meats.

MAYONNAISE À LA REMOULADE

1 cup plain mayonnaise	Parsley
1 Tbs. French mustard	Watercress
3 or 4 pickled gherkins, chopped	Chervil

Pound herbs in a mortar with some drops of lemon juice

Squeeze out the juice and add to mayonnaise mixed with mustard and the chopped gherkins.

MINT SAUCE

1 good handful mint, chopped very fine	2 cups veal or beef stock
1 Tbs. tarragon vinegar	Salt
1 tsp. sugar	Pepper

Put the chopped mint in a bowl; add vinegar and sugar. To this add the stock and mix all together. Stand in a saucepan of hot water on the fire and let it warm without boiling. If the mint boils it will be very bitter.

PARSLEY SAUCE

3 branches parsley	1 tsp. vinegar
¾ cup boiling water	1 tsp. chopped parsley
1 Tbs. melted butter	½ tsp. salt
1½ Tbs. flour	⅛ tsp. white pepper
1 egg yolk	2 Tbs. butter
1 Tbs. cream	

Wash parsley and cook in boiling water for 5 minutes. Mix in a saucepan the melted butter and flour and cook 1 minute. Strain the parsley water into this pan and stir until it comes to a boil, add chopped parsley and seasoning. Mix egg yolk with the cream and vinegar and add to the sauce with the 2 Tbs. butter. Briskly mix 1 minute and pour into a sauce bowl.

SAGE RELISH

4 Tbs. fresh sage leaves	⅛ tsp. cayenne pepper
2 Tbs. lemon peel, thin	1 Tbs. lemon juice
2 Tbs. salt	2 cups claret

Mix all together and steep in the claret for 2 weeks. Shake

well every day. Let stand a day to settle, then decant the clear liquid. Cork tightly and use about 1 Tbs. to flavor gravy or melted butter. Serve with roast pork.

SAGE AND ONION SAUCE

2 Tbs. onion, chopped fine	½ tsp. pepper
1 Tbs. fresh sage leaves	2 Tbs. fine bread crumbs
4 Tbs. water	½ cup stock
1 tsp. salt	

Put the chopped onion and sage in a saucepan with the water; simmer gently 10 minutes, then add seasoning and bread crumbs. Mix well; add stock and simmer 5 minutes longer and serve with pork or goose.

SAUCE PIQUANTE

2 Tbs. butter	1 bay leaf
2 onions	1 sprig parsley
1 carrot	Chives
2 shallots	1 Tbs. flour
2 cloves	1 Tbs. vinegar
A little stock	Salt
1 sprig thyme	Pepper

Chop all the vegetables and herbs; put them with the butter in a double boiler. When the butter is melted and turning brown, sift in the flour, stirring all the time; add a little stock and the vinegar; season to taste. Boil the sauce up slowly and put it through a sieve.

Serve with calf's head, brains, grilled trout, or braised cutlets.

SAUCE PRINTEMPS

3 Tbs. butter
2 oz. diced bacon
2 shallots, chopped
12 mushrooms, sliced
¼ cup brandy
1 cup claret
1 cup strong chicken stock
A few drops vinegar

1 Tbs. minced parsley
1 Tbs. minced chervil
½ tsp. minced chives
1 tsp. minced celery
A few tarragon leaves
A pinch of thyme
A few peppercorns, crushed
A few grains cayenne pepper
Salt

Fry the butter and bacon in an earthenware saucepan, together with the shallots and mushrooms. When the whole is a rich brown, pour on the brandy, set fire to it, and as the blaze dies down add the claret and chicken stock. Add herbs, spices, and salt. Let simmer very gently 15 minutes, strain, and cook another 4 minutes. During these 4 minutes, thicken first with a lump of butter, and then with the blood from the birds, which has been carefully saved in a bowl, and to which vinegar has been added to prevent congealing. Serve with quail, squab, grouse, or pheasant.

SAUCE RAVIGOTE (COLD)

½ Tbs. tarragon vinegar
1 hard-boiled egg yolk
1½ Tbs. olive oil
1 tsp. minced tarragon
1 shallot

1 stalk celery
½ tsp. parsley
½ bay leaf
1 clove

Chop egg yolk and add vinegar. Add oil gradually. Chop the tarragon, shallot, celery, parsley, bay leaf, and clove and add to sauce. Serve with cold fish.

SAUCE VINAIGRETTE

2 shallots, minced	1 Tbs. capers
2 small pickles, minced	¼ tsp. salt
2 sprigs parsley, minced	⅛ tsp. pepper
2 sprigs chervil, minced	2 Tbs. tarragon **vinegar**
2 sprigs tarragon, minced	4 Tbs. olive oil
½ tsp. minced chives	1 egg yolk, hard-boiled

Mix together well, mashing the egg yolk with a fork. Serve with cold asparagus, artichokes, etc.

SOUR CREAM SAUCES

RUSSIAN SAUCE

3 yolks of hard-boiled eggs	Paprika
1 cup thick sour cream	1 tsp. chervil, minced
Salt	1 tsp. tarragon, minced

Mash egg yolks very smooth. Stir into them the sour cream. Add seasoning and herbs.

UNCOOKED SOUR CREAM DRESSING

2 hard-cooked egg yolks	2 Tbs. lemon juice
Garlic	¾ cup sour cream

Rub bowl with cut garlic clove. Press egg yolks through sieve into bowl. Stir in lemon juice and sour cream. Beat until smooth.

COOKED SOUR CREAM DRESSING

1 cup sour cream	2 Tbs. sugar
½ tsp. dry mustard	½ tsp. salt
3 egg yolks	¼ cup vinegar

Mix mustard, salt, and sugar. Add the egg yolks and beat lightly. Stir in sour cream and vinegar. Cook in top of double boiler over hot water until mixture coats spoon. Chill before using.

TARTARE SAUCE

1 shallot	2 egg yolks
1 Tbs. capers	½ tsp. ground mustard
6 sprigs tarragon	1 tsp. wine vinegar
6 sprigs chervil	Salt
1 cup olive oil	Pepper
2 gherkins	

Chop shallot, capers, tarragon, chervil, and gherkins very fine and put them into an earthenware bowl with the raw egg yolks, mustard, and seasoning; stir in the vinegar, a drop at a time, and then the oil.

TOMATO SAUCE NO. 1

¼ onion	8 or 9 tomatoes, sliced (or
½ stalk celery	8 or 9 Tbs. conserve
A few leaves of sweet basil	and 1 cup hot water)
A bunch parsley	Salt
½ cup olive oil	Pepper

Mince the onion, celery, basil, and parsley; add olive oil, seasoning, and tomatoes. Boil until the sauce is as thick as cream, stirring occasionally, then strain through a sieve and serve with spaghetti, meat or egg dishes.

TOMATO SAUCE NO. 2

1 large can tomatoes	4 or 5 sprigs fresh basil
(or 4 cups stewed)	(or 1 tsp. dried)
4 onions, minced fine	Salt
1 clove garlic	Pepper

Cook onions in lard, take out garlic; add tomatoes and basil. Season; cover and stew slowly for 1 hour or until thick and thoroughly cooked.

TOMATO SAUCE NO. 3

4 large tomatoes, peeled and cut in pieces (or 2 cups canned tomatoes)
1 large onion, minced
½ green pepper, minced
1 clove garlic
1 canned pimento, cut into small pieces

1 sprig basil
1 sprig thyme
2 Tbs. butter (or 3 Tbs. olive oil)
1 tsp. salt
Few grains cayenne pepper
Paprika

Cook the onion, garlic, and green pepper in the butter or oil until yellow. Do not allow to brown. Remove the garlic; add tomatoes, pimento, herbs, and seasoning. Cook about 10 minutes and serve without straining. This is used with omelets, poached eggs, etc.

TOMATO CREAM SAUCE

1 cup white sauce, made from
2 Tbs. butter
2 Tbs. flour
1 cup milk
½ tsp. salt
Pepper
2 cups canned tomatoes

1 onion, minced
3 sprigs basil
Herb bouquet (celery tops, bay leaf, sprig thyme)
½ tsp. salt
¼ tsp. soda

Cook the tomatoes, onions, and herbs together for 5 minutes; rub through a strainer; add soda and combine with the white sauce. (For egg timbales, cornmeal or cheese soufflés, etc.)

TOMATO SAUCE MEXICAN

2 Tbs. butter
1 onion, chopped fine
1 chili pepper, cut in half
1 clove garlic
4 large tomatoes, peeled and cut into pieces (or 2 cups canned)

1 tsp. orégano [1]
1 green pepper, minced
Celery tops
1 tsp. Worcestershire sauce
¼ tsp. celery salt
1 tsp. chili powder

Cook onion, peppers, and garlic clove in butter 5 minutes.

[1] Wild marjoram.

Remove garlic; add tomatoes and celery and cook 15 minutes. Then add seasoning and herbs and serve without straining. (For omelets and other egg dishes.)

WHITE WINE SAUCE NO. 1
(with fine herbs)

1 Tbs. minced shallots	2 Tbs. butter
1 Tbs. minced mushrooms	1 Tbs. flour
1 Tbs. minced chives	½ cup white wine
1 tsp. minced parsley	Salt
½ cup white stock	White pepper

Simmer shallots and mushrooms in butter without browning. Add flour, stir well, then the stock and simmer 10 minutes. Add remaining ingredients; cook 3 minutes more and serve.

WHITE WINE SAUCE NO. 2
(with fine herbs)

4 Tbs. melted butter	1 Tbs. onion juice
1 Tbs. flour	Minced parsley
1 cup reduced stock	Juice of ½ lemon
½ cup dry white wine	Salt
1 Tbs. mushroom liquor	White pepper

Cream flour with 1 Tbs. butter; add reduced stock in which meat or fish has been cooked; cook until very thick. Thin with wine; heat and stir until smooth. Add remaining ingredients, beating in butter last.

For fish or warmed-over chicken.

CHAPTER VI

EGGS

Most egg dishes are immensely improved by adding herbs, and there is almost no limit to the amount or the number of varieties which may be used. The 'omelette aux fines herbes' is no longer the tasteless dish of tradition (American or English) in which the 'herbes' consisted of parsley and only parsley. Combine four or five sweet herbs, add, if fresh chives are not available, a very little minced onion or garlic to the butter in the pan, and you will have that work of art — a truly savory herb omelet. Plain scrambled eggs will be glorified if you add a little minced tarragon, basil, or sorrel or the same fine herbs used for omelets.

OMELETS

Directions for Making a French Omelet

Use an omelet pan of steel or iron, which should never be used for anything else. It should not be washed but wiped dry while *hot* with a paper towel or tissue.

Fresh eggs	Freshly ground pepper
Fresh butter	Fresh herbs
Salt	

Beat 4 or 5 eggs in a bowl with a fork; add ½ tsp. salt and ¼ tsp. pepper. Put 2 Tbs. butter in pan and when it smokes, pour in the eggs, beating them lightly as you do so. Stir the eggs while in the pan, and when it is beginning to set, tip toward you, scraping or lifting with a spatula toward the handle. Shape it a little, then roll it over to the opposite side until the outside is set, never letting it stick to the pan or get brown. Slide onto a hot platter and serve at once. The inside should be very soft — almost liquid — and the outside smooth. About 1 Tbs. minced herbs may be added to the eggs while beating or just at the last before the omelet is folded over. Serve at once or it will be spoiled.

Combinations of fine herbs for omelets:

Chives, parsley, chervil, basil, thyme.

Chives, tarragon, parsley.

Chives, chervil, sweet marjoram, thyme, parsley.

Fennel, chives.

A delicious 'green' omelet can be made with finely chopped fennel leaves, using about three times the usual amount of fine herbs, that is, for an omelet of from 4 to 6 eggs, use 3 Tbs. fennel.

SORREL OMELET

For an omelet of 6 eggs, take one good handful of fresh young sorrel leaves; wash and remove stalks and dry the leaves, then cut very fine with a knife or scissors. Make the omelet as usual, adding a half clove of minced garlic and a little chervil or parsley. Just before the omelet is done, spread the minced sorrel over and then turn. It should be rather thick so that, the inside being less cooked, the sorrel remains almost raw, which will give it a fresh acid taste pleasing to those who like sorrel.

The above combinations may be varied indefinitely.

OMELET
(*with chicken livers*)

4 chicken livers	1 tsp. minced chives
1 Tbs. butter	1 tsp. minced chervil or parsley
1 tsp. flour	2 Tbs. chicken or beef stock
Salt	2 Tbs. Madeira or sherry
Pepper	

Sauté the livers in butter, sprinkle over flour and seasoning. Stir well, add stock and wine and simmer 5 minutes. Add herbs and pour over omelet on platter.

OMELET
(*with kidney and mushrooms*)

6 lamb kidneys	2 Tbs. butter
6 mushrooms	1 tsp. flour
6 small cubes of salt pork	1 tsp. minced parsley
1 tsp. beef extract	1 tsp. minced chives
½ cup red wine	Salt
1 tsp. brandy	Pepper
1 medium onion, minced	

Put the wine in a saucepan and add the beef extract; reduce to one-half. Meanwhile wash the kidneys well and slice thin, removing all tough, stringy parts. Brown the onion lightly in the butter; skim out the pieces and put them in the wine. In the same butter brown the cubes of salt pork. Take them out and throw them away, then sauté the mushrooms lightly in the remaining butter. Sprinkle the flour over them and add the wine and let simmer gently. In another frying-pan melt 1 Tbs. butter and when sizzling hot put in the kidneys, which have been sprinkled with salt and pepper; stir them well. Brown, but do not let them cook long or they will be tough. Pour over the brandy and light it, then add the wine sauce and let them barely simmer while you make a 6-egg omelet. Just before the omelet is ready, add a small lump of butter, parsley, and chives to the kidneys. Spread over the omelet and turn. Serve on platter with the sauce poured around it.

SPANISH OMELET

Make either a French or puffy omelet and serve with Spanish sauce.

Sauce

4 large tomatoes, peeled and cut in pieces, or 1 cup canned	1 sprig basil, minced
	1 sprig thyme, minced
1 large onion, minced	2 Tbs. butter (or 3 Tbs. olive oil)
½ green pepper, minced	1 tsp. salt
1 clove garlic	Few grains cayenne pepper
1 canned pimento, cut into small pieces	Paprika

Cook the onion, green pepper, and garlic in the butter (or oil); take out garlic and add tomatoes, herbs, and pimento. Cook about 15 minutes; pour off excess liquid, season, and pour over omelet on platter.

SOUFFLÉS

Soufflés may be steamed in a double boiler. This method has one advantage over baking in that the time element is not so vital — the soufflé may be cooked 10 or 15 minutes more or less without injury if guests are late. Turned out on a platter it will not always keep its shape, but if completely covered with a sauce, the shape is not so important.

STEAMED SPINACH SOUFFLÉ

1 cup prepared spinach purée	Salt
¼ cup chopped fresh sorrel, **or**	Pepper
2 Tbs. minced chervil	Nutmeg
½ cup thick white sauce	¼ tsp. minced onion
3 eggs	

Mix the spinach with the white sauce, the minced onion, slightly beaten egg yolks, sorrel, and seasoning, stirring well. Fold in stiffly beaten egg whites and pour into a well-greased double boiler. Cover and steam 1½ hours. Turn out on platter and pour over the following sauce.

Sauce

½ cup white stock	1 piece of carrot
½ cup milk	½ bay leaf
2 Tbs. butter	1 sprig parsley
1 Tbs. flour	½ tsp. salt
1 hard-boiled egg, chopped	Pepper
1 tsp. minced onion	

Cook the butter and flour together with the onion about 5 minutes. Add the milk, which has been heated, the carrot, bay leaf, and parsley. Cook 10 minutes; add seasoning and strain. Add the chopped egg just before taking off the stove.

EGGS BROOKSIDE

Prepare a purée of spinach and arrange on a serving-platter, flattening it with a knife and dividing into individual portions. Sauté in a little butter as many slices of thin boiled ham as there are portions, and arrange on the spin-

ach. Poach the required number of eggs and put on the ham, then cover with Hollandaise sauce, with a little minced fresh tarragon sprinkled on each portion.

EGGS FLORENTINE

3 cups prepared spinach purée (or enough to cover bottom of shallow casserole)	1 tsp. minced tarragon or basil
Eggs	Grated Parmesan cheese
1 cup cheese sauce (Mornay)	Salt
1 tsp. minced parsley	Pepper
	Nutmeg

Spread prepared spinach on the bottom of the casserole and sprinkle with a little grated cheese. With a spoon make as many depressions or hollows as there are portions — slip into each an egg, then cover all with sauce Mornay, grate over some more cheese, and bake until eggs are set, 10 to 15 minutes. Serve immediately.

Sauce Mornay

½ cup white stock	1 piece carrot
½ cup milk	1 bay leaf
2 Tbs. flour	Parsley
2 Tbs. butter	Salt
2 Tbs. grated Swiss cheese	Pepper
1 tsp. minced onion	

(The stock may be omitted and ½ cup more milk added.)

EGGS MOLLET

Place eggs in deep rapidly boiling water, cover tightly. Remove immediately from the fire and let stand 8 minutes. Remove, dip into cold water, and set aside until thoroughly cold. Remove shells with great care, as the eggs will be soft.

If you wish to use them hot, leave them in the water 9 minutes. The cold eggs may be reheated, however, by steaming a few minutes.

EGGS MOLLET
(*in aspic*)

Cook as many eggs by the above method as you wish to
serve and chill thoroughly.

Directions for Making Aspic

1 qt. chicken or veal stock	A few grains cayenne pepper
2 Tbs. mixed chopped herbs	1 Tbs. tarragon vinegar
(thyme, marjoram, parsley,	2 Tbs. gelatine, soaked in
chives, and basil)	½ cup cold water
1 tsp. salt	2 egg whites, slightly beaten

Cook the stock with the herbs about 20 minutes; strain
and add the salt and pepper, vinegar, and gelatine. Cool,
then add the slightly beaten egg whites and the egg shells;
stir over the fire until boiling point, then allow to cook
without stirring 10 minutes. Strain through double cheesecloth over a fine strainer.

Take individual timbale molds, dip them in cold water,
and pour in each about 1 Tbs. of the liquid aspic, place in
icebox to harden, and when set arrange several leaves of
fresh tarragon on the jelly, pour in a few drops of the liquid
to set the tarragon in place, then place an egg in the center
and add a little aspic to set it. Then fill the mold with aspic,
place in icebox until cold and firm. Unmold, arrange on
platter with watercress or lettuce, and pour over each timbale 1 Tbs. green mayonnaise, adding some chopped tarragon and parsley.

This recipe may be varied by placing a thin slice of boiled
ham, cut to fit the mold, over the first layer of aspic; a little
liquid is added, the egg placed upon this and then filled to
the top with the aspic.

EGG TIMBALES
(with tomato sauce)

6 eggs
1½ cups thin cream
A little pepper
1 tsp. salt

½ tsp. onion juice
1 Tbs. each, of finely minced chives,
    parsley, or chervil, and thyme **or**
    summer savory

Beat the eggs well with the salt and pepper; add onion juice, cream, and the herbs. Pour into buttered timbale molds or cups, place in a pan of hot water, and bake in moderate oven until firm. Turn out on hot platter and pour the following sauce over them.

Tomato Cream Sauce

1 cup white sauce:
  2 Tbs. butter
  2 Tbs. flour
  1 cup milk
  ½ tsp. salt
  pepper

2 cups canned tomatoes
1 onion, minced
3 sprigs basil
Herb bouquet (celery tops,
    bay leaf, sprig thyme)
Pinch soda

Cook the tomatoes, onion, and herbs together for 5 minutes; rub through a strainer, add soda, and combine with the white sauce.

STUFFED EGGS
(with shredded cabbage)

6 hard-boiled eggs
Tarragon mayonnaise
½ tsp. mustard
1 tsp. minced chives

1 Tbs. minced tarragon
Salt
Pepper
Shredded cabbage

Cut the eggs in half lengthwise, take out yolks, mash with a little mayonnaise, mustard, salt, pepper, chives, and tarragon. Fill the egg halves with this mixture and serve on a flat dish with shredded cabbage which has been thoroughly mixed with tarragon mayonnaise thinned with cream. Pour a little of the mayonnaise over each stuffed egg and garnish with sprigs of fresh tarragon.

DEVILLED EGGS
(in casserole)

6 hard-boiled eggs	1 Tbs. minced herbs
Mayonnaise	(chives, tarragon, parsley)
½ tsp. mustard	½ lb. mushrooms
Salt	12 shrimps, or
Pepper	½ cup crabmeat

Cut the eggs in half crosswise, take out yolks, mash, and mix with a little mayonnaise, the mustard, salt, pepper, and minced herbs. Refill the egg whites and place in a well-buttered casserole or in individual ramikins which have been partially filled with a mixture of cut-up shrimps or crabmeat and the mushrooms sliced and sautéed in a little butter. Cover with cheese sauce, sprinkle with more minced herbs, and bake in hot oven 10 minutes.

Cheese sauce

2 Tbs. butter	½ cup grated cheese
2 Tbs. flour	Salt
1 cup rich milk	Pepper

Cook the butter and flour together, add milk and grated cheese; season and cook until thickened.

EGGS 'IN-A-HUDDLE'

1 zucchini squash	1 tsp. salt
2 Tbs. butter	¼ tsp. pepper
1 tsp. minced chives	Paprika
1 tsp. minced parsley	6 Tbs. milk
1 Tbs. minced marjoram	Pimentos
6 eggs	

Cut the zucchini into thin slices crosswise. The rind may

be left on or else lightly scraped. Melt butter in the frying-pan, add the zucchini and herbs. Sauté 8 minutes or until tender but do not burn. Beat the eggs very light, add salt, pepper, and milk. Beat 2 minutes more. Pour this over the zucchini and draw the mixture from the outside toward the center of the frying-pan until the eggs are set. If too moist, they may cook a few seconds longer. Sprinkle with paprika and garnish with a little cut-up pimento if liked, or the pimento may be added to the eggs and all cooked together.

EGGS RANCHEROS

1 cup Mexican tomato sauce
Eggs

Cover the bottom of a shallow casserole with the sauce. With a spoon drop in the raw eggs, sprinkling a little salt and paprika on each one. Place in oven until set and serve in same dish.

Mexican Tomato Sauce

1 onion, chopped fine	Celery tops
2 Tbs. butter	1 tsp. Worcestershire sauce
1 chili pepper, cut in half	¼ tsp. celery salt
1 clove garlic	1 tsp. orégano
4 large tomatoes, peeled and	1 tsp. chili powder
cut into pieces, or 2 cups	1 green pepper, minced
canned	

Cook onion, pepper, and garlic in butter 5 minutes. Remove garlic, add tomatoes and celery, and cook 15 minutes. Then add seasonings and herbs and serve without straining.

POACHED EGGS WITH HERBS

Poached eggs may be served on toast with a mixture of minced fine herbs and melted butter poured over them, or with a cream sauce, sprinkled with fine herbs.

SCRAMBLED EGGS

Add to the beaten eggs about 1 Tbs. of minced fine herbs in any combination desired; beat well, and cook as usual. This may be varied by using chopped sorrel instead of the herbs.

SCRAMBLED EGGS
(with tomato and basil)

Stir into the eggs while cooking 1 or 2 Tbs. thick tomato sauce, with a little minced fresh or dried basil.

EGGS COCOTTE
(with sorrel)

Make a purée by cooking 2 bunches of sorrel, or half sorrel and half lettuce or spinach, in ½ cup salted boiling water. Drain thoroughly, chop fine; add 1 Tbs. butter and a little cream and spread in individual small baking-dishes or cocottes. Drop in each an egg, cover with 1 Tbs. thin cream sauce, mixed with a little minced tarragon and parsley. Bake in hot oven until set.

EGGS PIMENTO

2 canned pimentos	½ cup finely chopped raw ham
1 fresh green pepper	1 tsp. salt
1 clove garlic	Paprika
1 medium-sized onion, minced	4 eggs
3 tomatoes	¼ cup olive oil

Cut the pepper, removing the seeds, and the pimentos in slices. Cook them with the onion and garlic in olive oil until soft, but do not brown. Remove the garlic, add the tomatoes, peeled and cut up, and the chopped ham. Simmer slowly about 1 hour, occasionally stirring and mashing the mixture, as it should be a soft purée. Break in one by one and without beating the eggs, stir quickly over the fire until the eggs are cooked.

CURRIED EGGS

2 Tbs. butter	1¼ cups meat stock or 1¼ cups
1 tsp. minced onion	water with 2 bouillon cubes added
1 Tbs. minced chives	6 hard-boiled eggs
1 clove garlic	½ tsp. lemon juice
2 Tbs. flour	2 tsp. curry powder
½ tsp. salt	Boiled rice

Melt butter. Add onion and garlic and cook until lightly browned. Take out garlic. Blend in combined flour, salt, and curry powder. Gradually add stock, stirring until thick and smooth. Cut eggs in quarters and add with lemon juice and chives. Heat through and serve with a ring of boiled rice, garnished with curried carrots.

CHAPTER VII

ENTRÉES, MACARONI, RICE, DRIED LEGUMES

LIST OF RECIPES

PASTES

Directions for Cooking Spaghetti

Have a large kettle of salted boiling water (1 tsp. salt to
1 qt. water) and put the spaghetti in without breaking.
Cook not more than 20 minutes; drain in colander and
return to kettle with sauce or butter and grated cheese,
mix well, using two forks, and serve on a very hot platter.

To Serve with Butter and Grated Cheese

For 1 lb. spaghetti use 6 Tbs. butter and 3 Tbs. grated Parmesan[1] or Romano cheese. Return spaghetti to kettle after draining; add butter, heat well, and then add cheese and mix well, using two forks. When serving, pass a bowl with more grated cheese.

TOMATO SAUCE FOR SPAGHETTI

1 large can tomatoes (or 4 cups stewed)	4 or 5 sprigs fresh basil (or 1 Tbs. dried)
4 medium-sized onions, minced fine	2 Tbs. lard (or 3 Tbs. olive oil)
1 clove garlic	1 tsp. salt

Cook onions and garlic in lard; take out garlic; add tomatoes, basil, and salt; cover and stew gently for an hour or until thick and thoroughly cooked.

SPAGHETTI
(with mushrooms and chicken livers)

4 livers	1 tsp. minced marjoram
8 mushrooms (or 3 Tbs. dried)	1 tsp. minced basil
2 Tbs. butter	4 Tbs. Marsala or sherry
2 Tbs. tomato sauce (or 1 Tbs. tomato paste)	Salt
1 tsp. minced chives	Pepper

Peel and slice mushrooms. Sauté them in 1 Tbs. butter, then add livers cut into small pieces, herbs, and tomato sauce (or paste thinned with 1 Tbs. hot water). Cook 3 minutes and add wine. If dried mushrooms are used, cover them with boiling water and soak 1 hour. Add the water to the sauce with the wine.

Put this sauce in a kettle with cooked and drained spaghetti; add 1 Tbs. butter and 2 Tbs. grated Parmesan cheese;

[1] Cheese should always be freshly grated.

reheat and mix well, using two forks, and serve on a very hot platter. Pass more grated cheese.

MACARONI LOAF (SICILIAN)

¾ lb. macaroni
1 lb. cold roast veal, minced
4 oz. boiled ham, minced
4 hard-boiled eggs, sliced
1 cup stock
Fine bread crumbs

1½ Tbs. minced sweet herbs
  (basil, parsley, chives,
  sweet marjoram)
1 tsp. salt
⅛ tsp. pepper
Grated Parmesan cheese

Break the macaroni into small pieces and cook 15 minutes in salted boiling water. Mix the veal, ham, eggs, herbs, and seasoning. Butter a mold and sprinkle bottom with bread crumbs, then put in alternate layers of macaroni and the meat mixture, sprinkling each layer of macaroni with grated cheese, until mold is full. Add the stock, sprinkle more bread crumbs, and bake in a pan of hot water in slow oven about 40 minutes. Turn out and serve with mushroom sauce or tomato cream sauce (page 85).

Mushroom Sauce

1 oz. dried mushrooms, or
  2 fresh mushrooms
4 Tbs. minced onion
1 tsp. minced parsley
4 Tbs. olive oil

1 Tbs. tomato sauce
¼ tsp. salt
2 cloves
A little pepper

Soak mushrooms in a cup of boiling water and let stand for 1 hour. Fry the onion and parsley in the olive oil about 3 minutes, stirring well. Press the water out of the mushrooms, saving the water, chop them with a knife; add to the onion and fry 1 minute longer. Add the water in which mushrooms were soaked, tomato sauce, chives, and seasoning and let boil slowly a half hour.

MACARONI LOAF OR TIMBALE

1 cup macaroni	1 cup bread crumbs
1 tsp. onion juice	1 Tbs. minced parsley
3 eggs	1 Tbs. minced celery leaves
1 cup milk	1 cup grated American cheese
1 Tbs. sweet red peppers, minced	1 tsp. salt
1 Tbs. green pepper, minced	

Cook macaroni in boiling salted water until tender; drain and chop. Scald milk, add bread crumbs, peppers, salt, cheese, onion juice, beaten eggs, and macaroni. Turn mixture into a buttered baking-dish and set in a pan of hot water. Bake a half to three-quarters of an hour in a moderate oven (350° F.). Serve with tomato cream sauce (page 85) flavored with basil, or any other tomato sauce.

NOODLE RING

6 oz. egg noodles (medium width)	1 Tbs. minced sweet marjoram or basil
1½ cups milk	4 Tbs. butter
¾ cup cracker crumbs	1 cup grated American cheese
1 tsp. minced onion	3 eggs
1 Tbs. minced green pepper	¾ tsp. salt
1 chopped pimento	⅛ tsp. pepper — Cayenne pepper

Cook the noodles without breaking in salted boiling water until tender; then drain. Scald the milk and pour over the cracker crumbs. Sauté the onion and green pepper in the butter, then add with chopped pimento to the milk and cracker crumbs, stirring well. Add the cheese and seasoning, then the beaten eggs, mixing thoroughly. Lay the noodles in a greased ring mold, keeping pieces fairly straight. Pour in cracker mixture, mixing carefully by separating noodles here and there with a knife to let sauce run through. Set in pan of hot water and bake 35 minutes at 350° F. Unmold and fill with creamed chicken or sweetbreads or any vegetable.

RICE

To Boil Rice

Wash rice in several waters until the last water is clear. Drain well and drop gradually into kettle of rapidly boiling salted (1 Tbs. salt) water so as not to stop the boiling. Boil hard without stirring about 15 minutes. Drain in colander and pour over 1 qt. hot water. Shake well and place in open oven to dry. (One cup raw rice makes about 3 cups when cooked.)

RICE TIMBALES OR RING
(*with saffron or curry*)

Boil 1 cup rice as above, but for 10 minutes only. Drain and finish cooking in 1½ cups chicken stock, to which may be added ¼ tsp. saffron or 1 tsp. curry powder. When the rice has absorbed the stock, pack in buttered individual timbales or a ring; set in pan of hot water in oven for 10 minutes. Turn out on platter and serve with creamed or curried meats or eggs.

With tomato

Finish cooking partly boiled rice as above but with 1½ cups of strained tomato juice instead of stock.

PILAF (OR PILAU)

1 cup rice, well washed	2 cups good stock or
1½ cups tomatoes, stewed	seasoned tomato juice or soup
and strained	¼ cup butter

Add the tomatoes to the stock and bring to a boil; add rice and steam covered until soft. Stir in butter with a fork, keeping uncovered to let steam escape.

RICE AND VEGETABLE PILAF

1 cup rice	¼ lb. salt pork, diced
½ green pepper, chopped	1 cup sliced okra
1 onion, chopped	3 cups chicken stock
2 cups fresh tomatoes, cut up	Salt
	Pepper

Fry pork in deep iron pan. When slightly brown add green pepper and onion and continue cooking until onions are a golden color. Add okra, tomatoes, and seasoning and cook until the quantity is well reduced. Boil rice in chicken stock for 12 minutes. Drain and add to first mixture. Cover pan and cook over a slow fire until rice is tender.

Wild rice may be used in this recipe, but must be cooked one half hour longer.

RICE RISTORI

1 cup rice	1 Tbs. minced parsley
2 cups veal or chicken stock	1 tsp. salt
2 oz. bacon, cut in small pieces	Pepper
½ small cabbage, chopped fine	Grated Parmesan cheese

Cook bacon in saucepan about 3 minutes; add the cabbage; cover and simmer slowly a half hour. Add salt, pepper, and parsley, then the rice and stock. Cover and cook about 20 minutes or until the rice absorbs the liquid, stirring frequently. Turn out on platter and sprinkle with grated Parmesan cheese.

SAFFRON RICE NO. 1

½ cup rice, thoroughly washed	½ cup olives (stones removed), chopped fine
2 cups beef stock or water	
2 onions, chopped fine	½ tsp. saffron
¼ green pepper (with seeds removed), chopped fine	2 Tbs. water
	Salt
1 pimento, chopped fine	Pepper

Fry the onion and green pepper in butter. Boil rice in

the stock, adding the strained saffron water, onions, green pepper, pimento, and olives. Season with salt and pepper and drain into a colander. Add a little butter and serve.

SAFFRON RICE NO. 2 (CREOLE)

1 cup rice	6 mushrooms
¼ tsp. saffron	2 Tbs. minced green pepper
3 Tbs. butter	1 tomato, cut in small pieces
1 Tbs. salt	1 onion, minced

Soak the saffron in 1 Tbs. water; add to boiling salted water and throw in rice. Boil 20 minutes; drain. Sauté the onion and peppers in 2 Tbs. butter, add the mushrooms and cook 2 minutes; then add the tomatoes and the rice. Cover and cook over low fire about 10 minutes. Add 1 Tbs. butter before serving.

SAVORY RICE

1 cup rice	2 tsp. parsley minced
3 Tbs. butter	2 tsp. summer savory or thyme, minced
2 onions, finely chopped	2 Tbs. marjoram, minced
1 clove garlic	2 Tbs. chervil, minced
3 cups stock or boiling water	½ tsp. salt

Cook onion in the butter 5 minutes. Add the rice and cook until the rice is slightly browned. Add salt, stock (or boiling water), and herbs, and cook until rice is tender and the liquid has been absorbed.

SPANISH RICE

1 cup rice	2 Tbs. lard
1 large onion, chopped	1 tsp. salt
1 pepper, chopped	Dash of cayenne pepper
1 cup canned tomatoes	A pinch of saffron
3 cups chicken stock	

Brown onion in lard, then add pepper and rice, which has

been washed well; stir constantly until the rice is slightly browned, then add stock, salt, cayenne, and saffron. Boil until the stock is quite absorbed by the rice. Arrange alternate layers of rice and tomatoes in casserole. Cook 15 minutes in moderate oven and serve in casserole.

RISOTTO WITH MUSHROOMS AND LIVERS

1 lb. rice	6 mushrooms
1 onion, minced	4 cups stock
6 Tbs. butter	2 Tbs. grated Parmesan cheese
3 or 4 chicken livers,	¼ cup Marsala
cut fine	Salt

Put onion into a 3-qt. saucepan and brown with the butter. Take out onion, put in rice and the Marsala. Reduce over a brisk fire, then add the stock and salt and boil hard so as to reduce in 18 minutes. Then take off the fire and season with 2 Tbs. butter and the Parmesan cheese, livers, and mushrooms, which have been sautéed, and some good gravy. Serve hot.

RISOTTO NO. 2

1 cup rice	2 to 4 cups boiling stock
2 large onions, chopped	2 Tbs. grated Parmesan cheese
4 Tbs. fresh butter	Small quantity powdered saffron

Fry onions in a casserole in 2 Tbs. butter, and when slightly brown throw in the rice adding more butter and stir continuously until the rice is brown. Then pour in part of the stock and continue to stir so that the rice does not stick to the casserole. See that it does not boil too hard; it should simmer only, and more stock or boiling water be added when necessary.

When nearly done, add rest of butter, cheese and the saffron dissolved in hot stock. Mix well all together and serve very hot with more grated cheese in a separate dish.

RISOTTO NO. 3

2 cups rice	⅓ cup white wine
1 onion, chopped	Stock
6 Tbs. butter	Grated Parmesan cheese
1½ oz. beef marrow	Salt

Cook the onion in the beef marrow and 3 Tbs. butter; when browned, put in the rice and the wine and enough stock to cook the rice. Before taking off the fire add 3 Tbs. butter and cheese. Serve with more grated Parmesan cheese passed separately.

DRIED LEGUMES

WHITE BEANS BRETONNE

2 cups white beans	3 small bunches parsley ⎫
2 qts. cold water	1 bay leaf or 1 sprig thyme ⎬ tied together
2 medium white onions, cut in halves	Celery leaves ⎭
½ lb. piece salt pork	2 Tbs. melted butter
1 tsp. salt	2 Tbs. flour
1 tsp. pepper	1 medium onion, chopped
	1 Tbs. minced parsley

Soak beans overnight in cold water. Drain and put in a saucepan with 2 qts. cold water, seasoning, onions, herbs, and salt pork. Cover and cook slowly 2 hours.

Heat in a saucepan the melted butter, add the chopped onion and flour, and cook 5 minutes, stirring constantly. Then strain all liquid from beans into this pan; mix well and boil 2 minutes.

Remove pork and herbs from beans, then add them to the sauce with the minced parsley. Mix gently with a wooden spoon and serve with rack of veal or pork.

CURRIED BEANS

2 cups red kidney beans	2 Tbs. butter (or olive oil)
½ lb. salt pork	1 Tbs. sugar
1 large onion, chopped	2 tsp. curry powder
1 apple, chopped	1 cup canned or stewed tomatoes
1 clove garlic	1 tsp. salt
1 sprig thyme	A few grains cayenne pepper

Soak the beans overnight; cook them, putting in a pinch of baking soda; boil about 10 minutes, then drain thoroughly; add 2 qts. boiling water, salt, and salt pork and cook about 2 hours or until tender.

Fry onion and apple in the butter or oil; add salt, pepper, sugar, and tomatoes. When all are well blended, add curry powder. Add the beans, mix well, and fill bean pot or deep baking-dish; cut up salt pork and mix with it, reserving some slices for the top. Then pour on some of the water in which beans were cooked, reserving the rest to add if the beans get too dry. Put in a slow oven and bake from 3 to 4 hours *covered*. (M. K. Doremus.)

KIDNEY BEAN PURÉE

2 cups kidney beans	1 clove
4 cups stock	Dash of cayenne pepper
1 slice salt pork, diced	Salt
1 onion, chopped	Pepper
1 sprig parsley	½ cup red wine
1 sprig thyme	

Soak beans in cold water overnight; drain. Cook all other ingredients except wine until beans are tender. Take out the clove and rub through a colander. Add wine, heat, and serve.

CANNELONI (STUFFED PANCAKES)

1 cup minced cooked chicken	½ tsp. salt
½ cup minced mushrooms	A little pepper
1 cup cream	½ tsp. minced fresh tarragon
2 Tbs. butter	2 Tbs. melted butter
1 Tbs. flour	Parmesan cheese
1 small white onion	

Cook the onion in 1 Tbs. butter; take it out and add rest of butter and the mushrooms. Cook 5 minutes; sprinkle with the flour, stir well. Add the chicken and the cream; cover and simmer gently until needed, stirring occasionally. Add tarragon and spread this mixture on the pancakes; roll them up and place in a buttered casserole or shallow pyrex dish; pour over them a little melted butter, sprinkle with Parmesan cheese, and put under broiler 2 or 3 minutes to brown.

The pancakes may also be arranged on a layer of spinach purée.

Recipe for French Pancakes

½ cup sifted flour	¼ tsp. salt
1 cup milk	2 eggs
1 tsp. sugar	1 Tbs. brandy

Sift the flour with the salt and sugar, make a hole in the center and break into it the eggs. Add a little of the milk and stir with a spoon until perfectly smooth, then add gradually the rest of the milk and the brandy, stirring constantly. Strain and let stand 1 to 2 hours. Use a heavy iron frying-pan about 5 in. in diameter. (There is one kind made especially for these pancakes.) Heat well; then sprinkle with salt, scour with tissue paper, and wipe clean with a towel, which will keep pancake from sticking. When pan is very hot, put in a small lump of butter, pour in 2 Tbs. of batter at one time, tilt the pan so as barely to cover the bottom.

When a delicate brown, turn over the pancake and brown the other side. Repeat until you have the required number.

CURRIED LENTILS ('DAL BHAT')

1 lb. lentils	1 cup bacon fat or ¾ cup butter
(preferably red)	6 Tbs. curry powder
2 qts. boiling water, salted	Boiled rice
4 large onions, sliced	

Soak lentils overnight in water to cover. Drain and cook in the boiling salted water until tender, about 2 hours. Press through sieve. Cook onion in bacon fat until lightly browned. Remove from pan and stir into remaining fat the curry powder, which has been mixed to a paste with 2 Tbs. cold water. Mix this with lentils. Serve over rice and top with onions.

LENTIL PURÉE
(*with sausages*)

2 cups lentils	1 tsp. salt
6 cups cold water	1 Tbs. butter
1 carrot, cut in pieces	1 Tbs. flour
1 branch celery ⎫	1 small onion, chopped
1 sprig parsley ⎬ tied together	12 sausages
1 sprig thyme ⎭	

Use red lentils if possible. Soak in water overnight. Drain and place in saucepan with 6 cups water, salt, and herb bouquet. Cover and simmer 2 hours. Take out bouquet and drain, reserving liquid.

Heat butter in saucepan; add flour and cook onion till light brown. Pour in all the liquor of the lentils, stir well, and boil 5 minutes. Then add lentils, mix, and boil 10 minutes more. Cover and keep hot.

Prick the sausages with a fork and fry 5 minutes on each side. Pile lentils around platter; arrange sausages on top.

POLENTA

2 cups coarsely ground
  white or yellow cornmeal
1 Tbs. butter
4 cups boiling water

1 tsp. salt
$\frac{1}{3}$ cup melted butter
$\frac{1}{2}$ cup grated Parmesan cheese
Paprika

Melt 1 Tbs. butter in the boiling water. Wet cornmeal with a very little cold water, add salt, then stir in slowly the boiling water. Bring to a boil, stirring continuously, until the meal is cooked and has lost its raw taste. It should be thick enough to make into a ball. Pour into layer-cake tins to cool. When cold, cut into rounds with cooky-cutter and put in a layer in the bottom of a pudding dish; pour over a little melted butter and the grated cheese, then more mush, cheese, and butter until the dish is full. Have the last layer of cheese sprinkled with paprika, and bake in a quick oven from 20 to 30 minutes.

POLENTA

(with sausages)

Prepare the polenta as in the above recipe. Cook 4 country sausages with a very little water; skin them and break into small pieces; then add 2 Tbs. stock, 1 Tbs. tomato conserve, and 1 tsp. minced basil. Arrange the polenta in a baking-dish with layers of the sausage and grated Parmesan cheese, dotted with bits of butter. Cover the top layer with grated cheese and butter and bake in hot oven about 15 minutes.

GNOCCHI ALLA ROMANA

2 cups milk (or half milk
  and half water)
$\frac{1}{2}$ cup white cornmeal
Salt

1 egg, beaten slightly
1 Tbs. butter
Several Tbs. grated Parmesan
  cheese

Let milk come to a boil, salt it, and add cornmeal gradually, stirring constantly so it will not become lumpy. Take off and add butter, cheese, and egg. Mix well and spread out on molding-board ¾ in. thick (or put in shallow tin). When cold, cut in squares, diamonds, or circles. Put layer of these in shallow baking-dish which has been buttered, sprinkle with cheese, and dot with butter. Repeat until dish is filled. Bake in oven until crust is well browned.

CHAPTER VIII

VEGETABLES AND VEGETABLE ENTRÉES

LIST OF RECIPES

CORN
  Savory Corn Pudding
  In Green Peppers
  Succotash

CUCUMBERS
  Pickled with Dill
  With Sour Cream and Chives

EGGPLANT
  À l'Italienne
  Provençale
  Stuffed

FENNEL (SWEET) OR FINOCCHIO
  Au Gratin
  Braised
  Stewed

GREENS
  Corn Salad (Mâche)
  Dandelion Greens
  Escalloped Dandelion Greens
  Good King Henry Purée
  Milkweed Shoots
  Mustard Leaves
  Purslane
  Young Turnip Tops

JERUSALEM ARTICHOKES
  Directions for cooking
  With White Wine

LEEKS
  Baked (au Gratin)
  Braised

LETTUCE
  Braised

OKRA
  Creole

ONIONS
  Cooked with Wine
  Stuffed Spanish

OYSTER PLANT
  With Fine Herbs

PARSNIPS
  Purée

PEAS
  Prepared the French way
  Purée
  Timbales

PEPPERS
  Stuffed
  Stuffed with Corn (see Corn)

POTATOES
  Boiled, New (with Fine Herbs)
  Mashed (with Mint or Water-
    cress)
  Mashed (with Mustard or Tarra-
    gon)
  Stuffed (with Fine Herbs)
  East Indian

SORREL
  Purée

SPINACH
  Purée
  Soufflé (with Chives)
  Soufflé (steamed)
  Spinach Benedict
  With Eggs and Marjoram
  Ring (filled with Vegetables or
    Mushrooms)

SQUASH
  Stuffed

SQUASH
  Zucchini (with Marjoram)
  Mexican (stuffed)

SWISS CHARD
  Puréed (with Creamed Midribs)

TOMATOES
  Baked (stuffed)
  Marseillaise
  On the Half-Shell

VEGETABLES
  À la King

'Pot Herbs,' they used to call them in the days when all vegetables and flowers too, were known as *herbs*. They were classified as pot herbs; green-leaf or 'sallet' herbs; sweet herbs and savory seeds; medicinal herbs or simples; fragrant, strewing, or 'nose' herbs. Vegetables and vegetable entrées are here presented as pot herbs or as vegetables prepared with the addition of sweet herbs. Delicious when fresh and well cooked, they supply the minerals and vitamins often missing in the average diet. Many people say they do not like vegetables, or at least are bored by them. There is some excuse for that distaste in a country where they are generally badly prepared — picked when too mature, marketed when too stale, eaten after too long cooking. Again the French — who excel not only in the cooking of vegetables but in their growing and marketing — consider no amount of trouble too great if the result is a superior product, and they exalt vegetable cookery to an art. Of course it is more work to prepare fresh vegetables than to open a can, but no canned product can substitute for such luxuries as fresh asparagus 'cut this morning,' young peas or corn boiled within a few minutes of picking, or fresh young spinach cooked in its own juice. These four vegetables in particular lose flavor, sweetness, and vitamins in the process of canning. Green vegetables should be cooked quickly in very little salted boiling water, lid off or, as in the case of spinach and other greens, in their own juices. Do not overcook or allow to stand in the water after they are done. If they have to wait for a delayed meal, take out of the water when half cooked, drain and keep hot, then reheat in a small amount of boiling water with butter added. The water in which vegetables are cooked should never be thrown away, as it contains the valuable mineral substances, and may be used in soups, sauces, or as vegetable stock. Vegetables which require long cooking, such as carrots, beets, and old string beans, may now be prepared very quickly in one of the new pressure cookers with a minimum amount of water. This method retains the flavor and no minerals or vitamins are lost.

In the following pages are many recipes for vegetable entrées which may be used as a 'main dish' for luncheon or supper. Prepared with cream and butter and served with rice, cheese, or mushrooms, they provide not only minerals and vitamins, but enough calories to satisfy the average appetite.

RECIPES

ARTICHOKES

BOILED

With a sharp knife cut off tips and remove hard outside leaves. Let stand in water with a little lemon juice. Cook in salted boiling water until tender; drain thoroughly. Serve hot with Hollandaise sauce flavored with chopped tarragon leaves, or cold with green mayonnaise, French dressing, or any other sauce desired.

'ALLA MILANESE'[1]

Put cooked artichokes into an earthenware casserole after greasing it well with fresh butter, then place a bit of butter in the center of each artichoke and sprinkle them with some finely grated Parmesan cheese. Cover and cook over a slow fire, taking care that the artichokes do not cook too long.

[1] Janet Ross, *Leaves from Our Tuscan Kitchen*. London: J. M. Dent.

Just before serving, pour some more melted butter over them and serve in the casserole.

STEAMED [1]

Remove the hard outside leaves of the artichokes, cut off tops but leave a little of the stalk. Then place them upright in a small saucepan with a little water, which must not quite cover the artichokes. Open out the artichokes and pour into the center of each a sauce made of pepper, salt, and olive oil. Then cover the saucepan and be careful to boil the water well so as to steam the artichokes thoroughly.

'À L'ITALIENNE'

Take small young artichokes, remove some of the outer leaves; trim them; cut off about an inch from the top and cut in half lengthwise. Do this beginning at the base and cutting through the leaves with a sharp knife. Soak in water and lemon juice for 20 minutes. Drain and dry. Cook in boiling chicken stock and, when tender, remove and drain. Pull out the hairy 'choke' and a few of the sharp inner leaves. Roll the chokeless artichokes in melted butter and freshly grated Parmesan cheese. Add ¼ cup of Sauterne and put in a shallow baking-dish in the oven. When quite hot, pour over a sauce of melted butter, chopped parsley, a little finely chopped shallot or chives, and the juice of a lemon. Serve in same dish.

ASPARAGUS

To Cook Asparagus

Use as fresh asparagus as you can get; trim, scrape, and tie in bunches, one to a portion. Cook uncovered in salted

[1] Janet Ross, *Leaves from Our Tuscan Kitchen*. London: J. M. Dent.

boiling water (1 tsp. to each quart of water) until tender, the length of time depending on the age and freshness of the asparagus. Remove and drain; place each portion on a piece of toast, removing the string.

Asparagus may also be steamed. After tying up the individual bundles, arrange them upright in a deep saucepan, packing them in tight so that they will stay upright. Fill halfway with salted boiling water and put the lid partly on. This method cooks the stalks while steaming the tender tips, which require less cooking.

With Butter Sauce

Pour off water in which the asparagus was cooked and save it for stock, leaving 2 or 3 Tbs. in kettle, to which add an equal amount of butter and a little cream. Shake a little to melt butter, pour over asparagus, and serve promptly. Never let asparagus remain in water after it is done; if it has to stand, dish it up and keep hot on top of stove.

With Hollandaise and Tarragon

Boil as in the above recipe, drain, and arrange on platter without toast. Pass Hollandaise sauce, to which a little fresh minced tarragon has been added.

Cold Asparagus

Boil, chill thoroughly, and serve with plain or green mayonnaise, sauce vinaigrette, or French dressing, with minced herbs.

ASPARAGUS EN CASSEROLE

Boil 2 bunches of asparagus according to directions. Drain and arrange on a platter or oval dish, one half on one side, one half on the other, so that the heads meet in the middle. Melt 4 Tbs. fresh butter; add 1 tsp. minced onion and 1 Tbs. flour and cook 5 minutes. Then add ¼ cup good stock or water in which asparagus was boiled, 1 bay leaf, 1 tsp. chopped parsley, salt and pepper to taste. Boil all together about 5 minutes; then add 3 yolks of eggs beaten; take off fire, stir well until slightly thickened; add a few drops of lemon juice and pour the sauce over the asparagus. Sprinkle with Parmesan cheese and put under broiler 1 minute. Serve at once.

BEANS

To Cook Beans

Green beans may be cooked more quickly if they are cut fine — the 'French' way — but the stringless variety, young and fresh from the garden, may be left whole, removing heads and tails, and tied in small bunches like asparagus. Pour over Hollandaise, or a butter sauce made with the remains of the water in which they were cooked, adding a little cream and an egg yolk if liked.

STRING BEANS
(with fine herbs)

Cook fresh young string beans in salted boiling water 15 minutes, then add a sprig of fresh summer savory and one of sweet marjoram. Finish cooking and serve with butter.

Canned string beans may also be improved by adding these herbs to the liquor as they are heating.

PURÉE OF STRING BEANS

2 lbs. string beans	2 sprigs summer savory
4 Tbs. butter	Salt
½ cup cream	Pepper
1 egg yolk	

Rather mature beans may be used. Cut them up without stringing and cook in salted boiling water with 1 Tbs. butter and the summer savory until quite tender. Mash through purée strainer and reheat with the rest of the butter and the cream mixed with egg yolk added at the last.

LIMA BEANS
(*in cream*)

Put fresh young lima beans in a saucepan and pour in enough boiling water to cover. Add butter, 1 Tbs. to each pint of lima beans, and salt to taste. Cook 6 minutes well covered, then remove cover, raise heat, and finish cooking quickly until water is absorbed. Pour in a little rich cream; let simmer 3 or 4 minutes, or keep hot in double boiler.

LIMA BEANS
(*with bacon*)

Cook 2 cups of lima beans in boiling salted water until tender. Drain off the liquid and add to the beans 2 cups of milk which has been slightly thickened with 1 Tbs. bacon fat mixed with 1 Tbs. flour. Add salt and pepper and place on a platter surrounded with slices of crisp fried bacon.

SUCCOTASH
(*See Corn, page* 128)

WAX BEANS

Cook in boiling salted water until tender. Drain, put in a saucepan or double boiler with butter and a little cream and freshly ground black pepper. Heat well and serve.

BEETS

To Boil Beets

Beets should be cooked whole in boiling water — the time varying according to the size and freshness of beets.

The tail should be left on and a little of the green stem, otherwise they 'bleed' and lose their color. Drain and pour cold water over them, then rub off skins. Very young beets fresh from the garden do not need to be peeled.

BEET GREENS
(with baby beets)

Cook young beet greens or 'thinnings' in salted boiling water, as little water as possible. Chop and add butter. Serve garnished with tiny whole cooked beets.

BEETS VIENNESE

Take 2 lbs. beets, boiled and sliced very thin. Make a sauce as follows:

6 Tbs. butter	⅛ tsp. pepper
1 tsp. finely chopped shallot	1 Tbs. flour
or white onion	½ cup red wine
⅛ tsp. cloves	½ cup stock
½ tsp. salt	1 tsp. sugar

Cook the shallot in the butter, add the cloves and the flour. Cook 2 or 3 minutes and add the stock. Bring to a boil, then add the wine, sugar, and seasoning. Heat up the sliced beets in this sauce and serve very hot.

BEETS
(with sour cream)

Boil the beets as usual; cut up and reheat with butter, salt, and pepper. Just before taking off fire add 4 Tbs. sour cream; stir well but do not allow to cook.

CABBAGE

To Boil Cabbage

Finely shred cabbage and cook in a small quantity of salted boiling water 5 to 7 minutes. Drain and reheat with butter, salt, and pepper.

GERMAN CABBAGE
(*with sour cream*)

Wash 4 cups shredded cabbage, cover with cold water, and let stand for 20 minutes to crisp. Drain, then cook in rapidly boiling water with 2 tsp. salt and 1 Tbs. chopped onion until tender, 5 to 7 minutes. Drain. Reheat with 2 Tbs. butter, 2 Tbs. sour cream, and 1 tsp. sugar.

RED CABBAGE

1 red cabbage	¼ cup vinegar (red basil is
4 tart apples, pared and sliced	good)
⅓ cup brown sugar	1 cup red wine

Shred cabbage very fine and put in heavy kettle with all the other ingredients except wine. Cover tightly and simmer for about 1½ hours. Add wine and continue to cook slowly for three-quarters of an hour longer.

CARROTS

CARROTS
(*in butter*)

Scrape the carrots lightly, cut in strips, or if small leave them whole. Place in a casserole with plenty of butter, a pinch of salt and pepper, and a small quantity of hot water. Cook very gently till the carrots are tender, the liquor much reduced, and the butter practically all absorbed. Sprinkle with finely chopped parsley, mint, or chervil, and serve on a hot dish.

CARROTS
(*with herbs*)

Wash two bunches very young carrots and put them in a saucepan with 1 Tbs. butter, a lettuce leaf, 2 Tbs. boiling water, and 1 tsp. sugar. Sauté them by shaking the pan and stirring them occasionally. They should cook in 25 minutes. Add 1 saltspoon salt, a dash of pepper and nutmeg, chopped parsley and tarragon, or mint, and serve without draining. One tablespoonful of cream may be added at the last.

GLAZED CARROTS
(*with mint or fine herbs*)

2 bunches carrots
¼ lb. butter
2 Tbs. mixed fine herbs, minced, or
  1 Tbs. fresh mint leaves, minced
2 Tbs. sugar

Slice and parboil the carrots in salted boiling water. Drain and put in double boiler with the butter and sugar. Cook until soft, add minced herbs or mint, cook 5 minutes longer. Turn out in serving-dish and sprinkle with more of the minced herbs or mint.

CURRIED CARROTS

1 cup curry sauce (See page 76. Omit coconut milk)
2 cups cooked carrots, cut in thick rounds
¼ cup cream
1 Tbs. butter

Sauté carrots in butter slightly, add curry sauce, and simmer a half hour. Just before taking off fire, add cream. Serve with ring of rice or curried eggs.

PURÉED CARROTS

Cook carrots by steaming until very tender. Mash through a coarse purée sieve; season with salt and pepper; add 1 Tbs. minced mint, butter, and a little cream. Reheat and serve.

CARROTS
(*with wine*)

2 bunches large carrots	Salt
¼ lb. butter	Pepper
2 Tbs. sugar	Nutmeg
1 cup dry white wine or 1 cup white wine vinegar	Paprika

Cut the carrots into thick slices and put in saucepan with half the butter, the sugar, and wine or vinegar. Simmer slowly about an hour, stirring occasionally. When the liquid is absorbed and carrots tender, add rest of butter, paprika, a little more salt, and grated nutmeg.

CARROT TIMBALES

1 qt. sliced carrots	1 tsp. minced chervil
2 Tbs. butter	2 eggs and 1 extra yolk
Boiling water or stock	Salt
Pinch of nutmeg	Pepper

Wash and scrape carrots, cut in slices lengthwise, and sauté in butter 10 minutes, stirring constantly. Cover with boiling water or stock and cook until soft. Drain and force through a purée strainer. Add eggs beaten slightly and the seasoning. Fill buttered timbale molds two-thirds full; set in pan of hot water, cover, and bake 15 minutes. Serve surrounded by green peas.

CAULIFLOWER

CAULIFLOWER À L'ITALIENNE

1 cauliflower	1 Tbs. minced parsley
2 Tbs. butter	1 Tbs. lemon juice
2 egg yolks	Salt
1 Tbs. flour	Pepper
6 mushrooms, sliced	Nutmeg
1 Tbs. cream	

Separate the cauliflower into flowerets and cook in salted boiling water until tender. Drain and arrange on pieces of buttered toast. Sauté the mushrooms in the butter, dredge with flour, add a little of the water in which the cauliflower was cooked (or 4 Tbs. white stock), simmer gently 5 minutes. Add egg yolks beaten with the cream, grating of nutmeg, seasoning and lemon juice, and parsley. Pour over cauliflower and serve hot.

CAULIFLOWER
(*browned with cheese*)

1 head cooked cauliflower	6 quartered browned almonds
¼ cup grated Parmesan cheese	2 Tbs. melted butter
¼ tsp. paprika	

Sprinkle cauliflower with cheese and paprika. Place under broiler grill until lightly browned for 5 to 8 minutes. When ready to serve, stick almonds into the flower and pour over melted butter.

CAULIFLOWER POLONAISE

Cook a cauliflower in 1 qt. of boiling water to which has been added 1 Tbs. salt and 1 cup milk. Boil until tender, place on a hot dish, and sprinkle with the following mixture, prepared while the cauliflower is cooking:

Yolks of 2 hard-boiled eggs, grated   2 Tbs. fine bread crumbs,
1 Tbs. minced chives   browned in butter
1 Tbs. minced parsley

Mix all well together, add 2 Tbs. melted butter, and pour over the cauliflower. Serve very hot.

CELERY

To Cook Celery

If celery is cooked in a vegetable stock, or water in which some other vegetable, such as carrots or onions, has been boiled, the flavor will be much improved. When it is tender and the liquid reduced, add a lump of butter rolled in flour and let simmer until the sauce thickens slightly.

Celery water should be kept for broth, or to mix with other vegetable stock.

The green leaves and outside stalks should be used to flavor soups and stews.

The leaves may be dried quickly in the oven, crushed, and kept in jars for flavoring.

BRAISED CELERY

2 bunches celery   1 cup chicken stock
3 Tbs. butter   Salt

Remove top leaves from celery. Cut into thick 3-in. pieces. Sauté in butter until light brown. Add stock, salt; cover and let simmer a few minutes. Remove celery to vegetable dish and pour the sauce left in pan over it.

Or take off outside stalks and top leaves of 3 bunches celery; parboil whole in salted boiling water, drain, and finish cooking in the stock.

CELERY

(cooked with cream)

Cut up celery in small pieces and cook in small amount of boiling salted water till water is almost absorbed. Add some butter and 1 Tbs. cream; reheat and keep hot in double boiler until ready to serve.

CELERY AU GRATIN (PARMIGIANO)

Take 6 large heads of celery; cut off the leaves; clean and cut in half lengthwise. Cook in boiling salted water 15 minutes; drain and lay in a shallow baking-dish; sprinkle with finely grated Parmesan cheese; pour melted fresh butter over them and a little cream and put into oven until they have taken a good color.

CHICORY

BRAISED CHICORY

2 heads curly chicory
1 carrot, minced
Chicken stock

2 Tbs. butter
2 small onions, minced

Parboil chicory in plenty of water. Drain and chop. Put the butter in a heavy saucepan, add onions, carrot, and chicory, and pour in stock to cover. Cover pan tightly and stew in oven for 1½ to 2 hours.

CORN

CORN SAUTÉ

Corn which is a little mature may be used for this recipe.
Parboil a dozen ears, cut off, and sauté with 1 Tbs. minced green pepper in 2 Tbs. butter. Add a little minced pimento just before it is done. Stir in 1 Tbs. cream; season and serve very hot.

SAVORY CORN PUDDING

2 eggs	¾ cup milk
2 Tbs. chopped green pepper	Salt
or pimento	Pepper
3 cups fresh corn pulp	Buttered bread crumbs
(or no. 2 can)	Grated cheese
2 Tbs. melted butter	

Beat eggs well; add green pepper (or pimento), butter, corn, milk, and seasoning. Pour into a buttered baking-dish and cover top with buttered crumbs mixed with an equal amount of grated cheese. Bake in a moderate oven until set and browned on top.

CORN

(*in green peppers*)

Make a thick cream sauce with 2 Tbs. butter, 2 tsp. flour, and ½ cup thin cream. Heat 1½ cups cooked corn pulp in this and fill cooked green peppers. Cover lightly with buttered bread crumbs and brown in oven 5 minutes.

SUCCOTASH

Boil 12 ears corn. Cut off with sharp knife and put in saucepan with butter, salt and pepper. Cook young fresh lima beans, drain, and add to corn with a little cream; heat well. There should be about one-third more corn than limas.

CUCUMBERS

PICKLED WITH DILL

Cover the bottom of a crock with green leaves, then with alternate layers of medium-sized cucumbers, fresh tops of dill, 3 peppercorns, 6 cloves, 6 allspice, and 1 tsp. mustard seed. Continue until the crock is nearly full, then pour over the following mixture: 1 cup salt, 1 cup vinegar, 1 gallon water. Fill to the brim, cover with green leaves, and let stand 2 weeks. Pack the pickles in jars, add more dill, heat the brine to a boil (adding more water), fill jars and seal.

CUCUMBERS
(*with sour cream and chives*)

Slice very thin and sprinkle with salt. Let stand an hour, then cover with sour cream mixed with minced chives, and serve in glass dish.

EGGPLANT
'À L'ITALIENNE'

1 eggplant, peeled, cut in thin slices	½ cup olive oil
Thin slices Italian bread	1 cup thick Tomato sauce, flavored with basil
Salt	1 cup grated Parmesan cheese

Sprinkle eggplant lightly with salt and put heavy plate on top; let stand several hours.

Fry eggplant and bread in hot oil. Place in layers in baking-dish alternately, covering each layer with the sauce and cheese. Cover top layer thickly with cheese and bake a half hour in quick oven.

Tomato Sauce

1 large can tomatoes	4 or 5 sprigs fresh basil (or 1 tsp., dried)
4 onions, minced fine	Salt
1 clove garlic	Pepper

Cook onions in lard with garlic; take out garlic; add tomatoes and basil. Season, cover, and stew slowly for an hour or until thick and thoroughly cooked.

PROVENÇALE

2 large eggplants	2 shallots (or 1 small onion)
4 Tbs. butter	Bread crumbs
Olive oil	Grated Parmesan cheese
4 Tbs. minced salt pork	1 clove garlic
6 mushrooms, cut into small pieces	1 Tbs. minced parsley

Cut the eggplants in two lengthwise and fry in oil until soft. Meanwhile cook the salt pork, minced shallots, garlic, and mushrooms in the butter, about 10 minutes. Remove garlic and drain the eggplants, scoop out the soft part with a spoon, chop, and add to the mixture in saucepan. Season with salt and pepper to taste; add parsley, fill eggplant shells, place them in a shallow casserole, sprinkle with bread crumbs and cheese, pour over a little olive oil, and brown in oven.

STUFFED EGGPLANT

Cook 1 medium-sized eggplant in boiling water for 25 to 30 minutes or until tender. Cut in half lengthwise and scoop out the center, leaving a shell ½ in. thick. Sprinkle inner surface with ½ tsp. salt. Mash the pulp, combining it with the following:

½ cup chopped nutmeats	1 Tbs. chopped parsley
¼ tsp. marjoram	1 Tbs. onion juice
⅛ tsp. pepper	1 egg, beaten

Heap the shell with this stuffing. Place in greased baking-pan and bake in moderate oven (350° F.) about 1 hour. Baste 2 or 3 times with ¼ cup water combined with 2 Tbs. melted butter.

FENNEL ('FINOCCHIO')

FENNEL PARMIGIANO

Wash the fennel bulbs thoroughly and cut each in half. Cook in salted boiling water until tender. Drain and arrange in a shallow baking dish, pour over a little melted butter, add salt and pepper, and cover with grated Parmesan cheese. Add 1 Tbs. cream and bake in oven till light brown.

BRAISED FENNEL

2 fennel bulbs	1 cup chicken stock
3 Tbs. butter	

Remove tops; cut bulbs into thick 3-in. pieces. Sauté lightly in butter. Add stock, cover, and let simmer until tender. Remove fennel to vegetable dish and pour the sauce left in pan over it.

CREAMED FENNEL

1 Tbs. butter	1 qt. water
1 Tbs. lemon juice	1 tsp. salt
4 peppercorns	

Put butter, lemon juice, salt, and peppercorns in the water and bring to a boil, stirring well. Wash the fennel bulbs, trim off tops and outside leaves, and cut in thick slices. Put in kettle and simmer slowly until tender. Drain and reheat in double boiler with butter and a little cream, adding paprika, a dash of nutmeg, and a few finely chopped fennel leaves.

GREENS

CORN SALAD (MÂCHE)

Used alone or mixed with other greens, for salad.

DANDELION GREENS

After washing thoroughly, cook in boiling water 5 minutes. Drain and throw away water, and put in another pot of boiling water with salt. Cook 10 minutes. Drain and chop fine; add butter and a little cream and serve with chopped hard-boiled egg.

ESCALLOPED DANDELION GREENS

2 qts. dandelion greens	1 beef bouillon cube
1 cup water	¼ cup grated cheese
¼ tsp. salt	¼ cup buttered bread crumbs
2 Tbs. butter	Pepper
1½ Tbs. flour	Paprika
2 cups hot milk	

Cut off the roots and imperfect leaves from young, tender dandelions. Wash thoroughly and separate leaves. Cook until tender, about 25 to 30 minutes, removing cover after 10 minutes. Drain, add seasoning, and chop fine.

Melt butter in top of double boiler, blend in flour, and add milk in which bouillon cube has been dissolved, stirring constantly. Place cooked dandelions in a greased casserole, cover with the white sauce, and spread over top grated cheese which has been combined with the bread crumbs. Bake in a moderate oven (350° F.) about 20 minutes or until top is well browned.

GOOD KING HENRY PURÉE

Wash well, tie up in small bunches with a sprig of mint in each bunch, put into boiling water, and boil fast for a half hour. Drain thoroughly, chop fine, and reheat with 2 Tbs. cream sauce. (See Spinach Purée, page 141).

MILKWEED SHOOTS

Tips of young milkweed cooked in boiling salted water and served with butter like asparagus.

MUSTARD LEAVES

Young mustard leaves cooked alone or mixed with other greens, or mixed in a green salad.

PURSLANE

Cooked like spinach, or cold in salad.

YOUNG TURNIP TOPS

Prepared like spinach purée.

JERUSALEM ARTICHOKES

Directions for Cooking

Never peel Jerusalem artichokes. They should be boiled or steamed in their skins and then peeled and served. If the water in which they have been boiled is kept it will become a thick jelly when cold, and the flavor is delicious. It makes a good foundation for artichoke soup. Another method is to parboil and then bake them. They may be peeled and sliced when they are cold and served with a French or mayonnaise dressing for salad.

JERUSALEM ARTICHOKES
(*with white wine*)

1 onion, chopped	1 tsp. salt
1 Tbs. butter	¼ tsp. pepper
6 Jerusalem artichokes	⅛ tsp. nutmeg
1 clove garlic	1 cup white wine
Herb bouquet	

Put onion into saucepan with butter and cook slowly until light brown. Add artichokes peeled and quartered, then the garlic, seasoning, and herb bouquet. Keep covered and simmer 15 minutes, very slowly, shaking the pan from time to time to keep the contents from catching on the bottom. Remove garlic and herb bouquet and add wine and a little hot water if needed. Continue cooking slowly until artichokes are done.

LEEKS

BAKED LEEKS AU GRATIN

Clean, blanch, and cook the leeks in boiling water. Then sauté in butter and place in a shallow baking-dish which has been sprinkled with a mixture of grated bread crumbs, chopped parsley, 1 Tbs. minced herbs (thyme, marjoram, chives), and the grated rind of a lemon. Cover with a thick white sauce. Sprinkle on the top a mixture of half bread crumbs and half grated Parmesan cheese; dot with small bits of butter and brown in oven.

BRAISED LEEKS
(*in casserole*)

6 leeks	1 sprig thyme
6 Tbs. butter	1 sprig marjoram
2 cups stock	1 sprig parsley
6 peppercorns	1 bay leaf
Salt	

Clean leeks thoroughly and soak in salt water. Cut in

two lengthwise; put them in a shallow casserole, cover with water, bring to a boil, and cook 3 minutes; then drain and return to casserole. Add butter, salt, peppercorns, and herbs (in a muslin bag). Fry all together for 10 minutes, then add 1 cup stock and cook very slowly with the lid on for 1½ hours. Dish the leeks on squares of buttered toast. Strain the liquor, remove all fat, boil till reduced one half, and add the rest of the stock. Pour over the leeks and serve in casserole.

LETTUCE

BRAISED

Wash lettuce, remove faded leaves, and cut off the roots. Tie the tops together, lay the lettuces side by side in a baking-pan, and pour in 1½ in. of chicken or veal stock. Cover the pan and put in a moderate oven for a half hour, adding more stock or water when necessary. Place a fork under the middle of each lettuce, raise and drain, and lay them doubled up on a hot dish. Season the gravy in the pan with butter, salt, and pepper; thicken with an egg yolk, and pour it over the lettuce. Serve hot.

OKRA

OKRA CREOLE

2 doz. okras	1 Tbs. butter
2 medium tomatoes	½ tsp. minced parsley
(or ½ cup canned)	Salt
½ green pepper, minced	Pepper
1 onion, minced	Cayenne
¼ clove garlic	

Wash okras and cut off ends. Put in saucepan with butter, onion, garlic, and green pepper and cook about 10 minutes. Remove garlic; add tomatoes cut up into small pieces and the juice, seasoning, parsley, and the okras and simmer 20 minutes.

ONIONS
(*with wine*)

18 small white onions	1 Tbs. minced chives
1 qt. stock	(or onion tops)
½ cup white wine	1 Tbs. minced parsley
1 Tbs. butter	½ tsp. salt
1 Tbs. flour	⅛ tsp. pepper
	Dash of cayenne pepper

Put onions into cold water and peel. Put them in sauce-pan with stock and cook slowly 1½ hours or until soft. Drain in colander and save stock. Cook butter and flour in frying-pan; add ½ cup of the onion broth, seasoning, and wine; boil up once and add onions; simmer 10 minutes, add chives and parsley and serve.

STUFFED SPANISH ONIONS
(*six Spanish onions*)

1 Tbs. butter	1 cup dairy cheese, cut
1 Tbs. flour	into pieces
1 cup thin cream or milk	4 Tbs. cracker crumbs
Salt	1 egg
Pepper	Worcestershire sauce

Parboil the onions and scoop out some of the center part. Into each onion put 1 Tbs. of sauce and bake brown in a quick oven. To the remainder of the sauce add a little thick cream and heat. Pour this over the onions and serve. Or onions may be stuffed with the following mixture:

Sauté a little minced onion and green pepper in 1 Tbs. butter. When slightly cooked add 1 cup soft bread crumbs ½ cup finely minced cold left-over meat, salt and pepper Heat and add chopped sweet herbs, chervil, parsley, thyme basil, or tarragon. Bake slowly for 1 hour.

OYSTER PLANT
(with fine herbs)

6 stalks oyster plant	1 tsp. summer savory, minced or
2 Tbs. butter	1 tsp. basil
1 tsp. parsley, minced	Lemon juice
1 tsp. chives, minced	Salt, pepper

Wash and scrape the oyster plant and soak in cold water with a little lemon juice. Cut in slices and cook in salted boiling water until tender. Drain and fry lightly in the butter. Add herbs and seasoning, stirring well. Place in shallow casserole, heat in oven and serve in same dish.

PARSNIPS

PURÉE OF PARSNIPS

6 or 8 parsnips	1 Tbs. flour
1 cup milk	½ tsp. salt
2 Tbs. butter	⅛ tsp. pepper

Cut up parsnips and boil in water till they are soft enough to mash. Drain and mash through colander. Melt 1 Tbs. butter in saucepan, cook with flour without browning; add milk but do not boil. Add parsnips, seasoning, and rest of butter. Stir well and serve with meat.

PEAS

GREEN PEAS
(cooked the French way)

2 or 3 lettuce leaves	¼ lb. sweet butter
1 small white onion	1 Tbs. sugar
1 sprig parsley	4 cups shelled young peas
½ cup cold water	Small pinch of salt

Tie onion and parsley up inside the lettuce. Put the butter in a heavy saucepan; add sugar, lettuce, and peas. Pour over the water; place on a very hot fire and bring quickly to a boil; reduce heat quickly and cover tightly. Let the peas cook slowly until tender; then add salt, and serve in their juice.

GREEN PEA PURÉE

3 cups peas (or 1 can)	4 Tbs. butter
3 tsp. sugar	1 cup water
½ tsp. grated onion	½ cup cream
1 tsp. minced parsley	½ tsp. salt
1 tsp. minced mint or	Pepper
2 Tbs. chopped lettuce	

Cook peas in double boiler with water and all other ingredients except cream and seasoning. When thoroughly soft, mash through coarse strainer, add cream, salt and pepper, and serve with sausages, or alone as vegetable. Mature peas may be used for this recipe.

PEA TIMBALES

2½ cups green peas	1 tsp. sugar
(or 1 can)	⅛ tsp. pepper
2 eggs	¼ tsp. grated onion
2 Tbs. melted butter	1 tsp. minced mint leaves
½ tsp. salt	1 tsp. minced parsley

Use peas that are a little mature and cook in double boiler with ½ cup cold water, sugar, and onion until soft enough to rub through a sieve. Add the eggs well beaten, the seasonings, butter, mint, and parsley. Turn into buttered timbale molds; set in pan of hot water; cover with buttered paper and bake in moderate oven until firm. Serve with creamed young carrots flavored with mint.

PEPPERS

STUFFED GREEN PEPPERS

Fry 6 medium green sweet peppers for 1 minute in boiling

fat; drain, peel, and cut off the ends, keeping them to use as covers. Remove the insides and fill them with forcemeat made of

Minced fresh pork	½ saltspoon grated nutmeg
1 tsp. salt	½ saltspoon powdered thyme
1 saltspoon pepper	

Put on the ends, lay the peppers in a well-oiled baking-dish, add a little olive oil, and put in a moderate oven to bake for 15 minutes. Turn them onto a hot dish and serve with ½ cup velouté sauce, with a little Marsala added.

Velouté Sauce

1 lb. knuckle of veal	2 carrots
Fowl scraps	1 onion
2 or 3 slices of ham	1 cup veal stock
Salt	2 or 3 shallots
Pepper	12 mushrooms
Herb bouquet	

Put the knuckle of veal and any scraps you have of fowl into a well-buttered saucepan with the ham, carrots, onion, and stock. When stock is reduced add the mushrooms, shallots, seasoning, herbs, and enough veal stock to cover the meat. Boil, skim off the fat, and let simmer for 1½ hours. Thicken with 1 Tbs. butter and 1 Tbs. flour.

POTATOES

BOILED NEW POTATOES
(with fine herbs)

Cook very small new potatoes in their skins in salted boiling water. Drain and sauté (without peeling) in butter, with minced herbs — parsley, chives or chervil, and basil.

MASHED POTATOES
(with mint or watercress, mustard or tarragon)

To 2 to 3 cups of hot mashed potatoes add 3 Tbs. butter, pepper and salt, pinch of cayenne, and ½ cup cream. Mix thoroughly by beating with a fork or wooden spoon; add 1 Tbs. chopped watercress or garden cress — or mint — or young mustard leaves. Mix well and serve very hot. A little minced fresh tarragon may be added.

STUFFED POTATOES
(with fine herbs)

Bake large potatoes; cut a slice off top or cut in two lengthwise. Take out inside of potato with spoon; mash with fork, adding butter, salt, and pepper, 1 Tbs. hot milk to each potato, and minced fine herbs (any combination desired). Fill the shells, top with grated Parmesan cheese, and bake in hot oven till brown.

POTATOES EAST INDIAN

4 boiled potatoes
4 Tbs. butter
2 shallots, chopped, or
   1 small white onion
1 clove garlic
1 tsp. grated lemon peel

1 tsp. minced parsley
1 tsp. turmeric, or
   ½ tsp. curry powder
1 pinch nutmeg
Salt
Pepper

Melt butter with garlic. Remove garlic, and fry shallots. Then add potatoes cut up and rest of ingredients except curry. When done, sprinkle with the curry or turmeric.

SORREL

PURÉE

Cut the stalks off 2 bunches sorrel, wash well, drain, and chop with 2 heads of well-washed lettuce (or spinach) and a small bunch of chervil. Put all into a saucepan and stir over a hot fire for 3 minutes; then place in the oven until well dissolved. Add 3 Tbs. butter, stir until it bubbles, add 1 cup good stock, and cook for 5 minutes. Good served with eggs mollet or poached eggs.

SPINACH

PURÉE

Pick over spinach (about 3 lbs.) and remove coarse stems and roots; wash thoroughly in several waters and cook covered, in own juice, not longer than 10 minutes (or less if spinach is very young and fresh). Add a little salt at the last. Drain and chop fine and press out the water, which should be kept for soup. Cook in a saucepan 2 Tbs. butter, 1 Tbs. flour, and ½ tsp. minced onion. Add the chopped spinach, stir well; add a dash of nutmeg, freshly ground pepper, and a little cream and reheat.

SPINACH SOUFFLÉ
(with herbs)

4 eggs	1½ Tbs. finely chopped chives
⅓ cup cooked	4 Tbs. light cream
chopped spinach	Salt
1 Tbs. sweet marjoram,	Paprika
minced	

Separate eggs. Beat yolks well. Add spinach, salt, paprika, chives, marjoram, and cream and mix thoroughly. Beat whites until stiff. Fold in; bake in casserole in moderately hot oven (375° F.) until fluffy.

STEAMED SPINACH SOUFFLÉ

1 cup spinach purée	1 tsp. marjoram (optional)
1 cup thick cream sauce	3 egg yolks, beaten
1 Tbs. chopped chervil or sorrel	3 egg whites, beaten

Put in well-greased double boiler and steam at least 1½ to 2 hours. Serve on platter with a cream sauce with chopped hard-boiled egg, minced chives, chervil, and marjoram.

SPINACH BENEDICT

Make a purée of spinach. Arrange on a platter in individual servings with a piece of thin sautéed boiled ham on each portion. On each piece of ham place a poached egg and cover with Hollandaise sauce. Sprinkle with chopped fresh tarragon.

SPINACH
(*with eggs and marjoram*)

Clean and wash the spinach well before cooking. Drain off the water; chop and put the spinach in a saucepan with some butter and salt to taste. After it has cooked for 15 minutes pour over it 2 or 3 well-beaten-up eggs with a little grated cheese and a few leaves of marjoram. Stir well and never allow it to boil or the eggs will set. Serve hot with croutons fried in good olive oil.

SPINACH RING
(*filled with vegetables or mushrooms*)

Prepare spinach as for a purée; add 2 eggs, the whites beaten separately and folded in. Pour into a ring mold, set in a pan of hot water, and bake in a moderate oven 20 minutes. Unmold and fill center with creamed mushrooms, or any creamed vegetable such as celery or carrots. It may also be served with Hollandaise sauce.

SQUASH

STUFFED SQUASH

6 small summer squash (scallop variety)

Sauce

1 Tbs. butter, cooked with	4 Tbs. cracker crumbs
1 Tbs. flour	1 egg
1 cup thin cream or milk	Worcestershire sauce
Salt	1 Tbs. minced marjoram (or
Pepper	basil)
1 cup dairy cheese, cut into pieces	1 tsp. minced chives

Cut off the hard stems of squash and parboil. Cut out a round disk from the top and scoop out some of the contents. Into each squash put 1 Tbs. of sauce and bake brown in a quick oven. To the remainder of the sauce add a little thick cream and heat. Add herbs and pour over the squash.

ITALIAN SQUASH ('ZUCCHINI')
(fried with marjoram)

One zucchini for each person	1 Tbs. olive oil to each zucchini
1 clove garlic	Salt
Sweet marjoram	Pepper

Slice young zucchinis very thin without peeling. Heat 2 Tbs. oil, add crushed garlic clove, fry until light brown, and remove. Cover bottom of frying-pan with slices of zucchini and slowly fry on one side. Season and push to one side of pan to keep hot and finish cooking; add a few sprigs of sweet marjoram, then in the empty part of the pan add more oil and fry more slices. Season and place under those already fried, repeating till all are done. The pan must be a wide one, with the heat centered under the part where the active frying is done.

MEXICAN STUFFED SQUASH

2 large crook-necked squashes	1½ cups stale bread cubes
3 cups left-over meat	1 egg, lightly beaten
1 Tbs. chili peppers	½ cup catsup
2 Tbs. green peppers	1 small onion
1 tsp. orégano	2 tsp. olive oil (or other fat)
(or 1 Tbs. fresh basil)	2 tsp. salt

Wash and parboil the whole squash until outside rind may be pierced with a fork (about a half hour). Cut in half lengthwise, remove the seeds, and stuff with the meat mixture, which has been topped with bread crumbs.

To prepare meat mixture, fry the onion to a light brown, add the ground meat and other seasonings. The bread cubes may be toasted or fried. Add egg as a binder.

Cover with bread crumbs which have been tossed in melted butter and brush the cut surfaces of the squash with melted butter so that it will brown. Bake in a 400° F. oven for about half an hour, or until slightly browned.

SWISS CHARD

PURÉED
(*with creamed midribs*)

1 qt. cooked greens	1 tsp. salt
1 cup cream sauce	Pepper to taste
1 Tbs. bacon drippings	
or butter	

Chard may be prepared in the same way as spinach, or the stem may be prepared like asparagus, either by cutting into 4-in. pieces and tying into small bunches before boiling, or by cutting into ½-in. pieces and creaming.

The greens should be stripped from the thick midrib, then

steamed or boiled like spinach tops. Cover the thick mid-rib (cut into ½-in. pieces) with boiling water and boil for 35 to 40 minutes, or until tender. Then drain and heat in the cream sauce, which is made as usual. The greens are drained, chopped and seasoned with salt, pepper, and bacon drippings or butter, and put in the center of a dish. Place around them the creamed midribs.

To get 1 qt. cooked greens, use 3 qts. of the fresh.

TOMATOES

STUFFED BAKED TOMATOES

Cut out centers of six large tomatoes. Sauté a little minced onion and green pepper in 1 Tbs. butter. When slightly cooked, add 1 cup soft bread crumbs, salt, pepper, and the pulp of tomatoes. Heat and add chopped sweet herbs (chervil, parsley, thyme, basil, or tarragon). Fill the tomatoes with this mixture; put in a little butter on the top of each; bake for 1 hour in pan set in another pan of water.

TOMATOES 'MARSEILLAISE'

6 large tomatoes	2 chopped anchovies
½ tsp. minced chervil	Fine bread crumbs
½ tsp. minced parsley	Salt
½ tsp. minced basil	Pepper
½ clove garlic, chopped	

Cut tomatoes in half lengthwise; season with salt and pepper. Mix together the herbs, garlic, and anchovies. Arrange tomatoes in a buttered shallow casserole or pyrex dish; divide the chopped mixture over them. Sprinkle with fine bread crumbs, baste lightly with olive oil, set in oven for 15 minutes, and serve in same dish.

TOMATOES ON THE HALF SHELL

6 solid tomatoes	½ tsp. salt
1 cup milk	Pepper
1 Tbs. flour	Minced tarragon or basil
1 Tbs. butter	

Cut tomatoes in halves, put them in a pan, dust with salt and pepper, and put a tiny bit of butter on each piece. Bake until soft but not broken, and arrange on a hot platter. Add flour to the pan and cook 5 minutes, then add milk, stirring well until it boils. Then add butter, seasonings, and herbs and pour over the tomatoes.

VEGETABLES

À LA KING

Grilled tomatoes
2 hard-cooked eggs, cut into quarters
A few cooked string beans, peas, car-
    rots and/or any left-over vegetables

Cut firm tomatoes into thick slices and fry lightly in butter. Arrange on platter and pour over the sauce with the hard-boiled eggs, then add vegetables in spoonfuls around the platter.

Sauce

1 Tbs. butter	Few grains cayenne pepper
1 cup mushrooms sliced	1½ cups milk
1 Tbs. green pepper, minced	1 Tbs. minced parsley
2 Tbs. flour	1 Tbs. pimento, cut into
½ tsp. salt	small pieces
½ tsp. celery salt	Tarragon
1 cup chicken stock	

Melt butter, add mushrooms and green pepper. Stir and cook 5 minutes. Mix flour and seasonings; add to pan. Add parsley, tarragon, and pimento.

CHAPTER IX

SALADS — SALAD HERBS AND SALAD VEGETABLES

LIST OF RECIPES

Orange
  With Watercress
  With Romaine
Parsnip
Potato Salad
Russian Salad
Spinach Salad
Spring Salad

Tomatoes
  With Lettuce
  With Avocados
  Sliced (French method)
Tomato Jelly (Recipe for)
Vegetable Salad
Watercress
  With Orange
Zucchini (Italian Squash)

> Salad refreshes without fatiguing and strengthens without irritating.... It renews one's youth.   BRILLAT-SAVARIN

The word 'salad' (Spanish *ensalada*, Italian *insalata*) is derived from *sal*, meaning salt, and, until it was corrupted by the modern school of tea-room cookery, denoted only such greens and vegetables — salad herbs — as could be eaten with salt and a seasoned mixture of oil and vinegar.

This discourse of 'sallets,' then, will ignore all decorative arrangements — half a canned pear on a leaf of lettuce, topped by a dab of whipped cream and a cherry or marshmallow, or a slice of pineapple with a spoonful of cream cheese and a ring of raw green pepper.

Our interpretation of salad approaches more nearly to the French, Italian, or Continental, the making of which requires a large pottery or wooden bowl, with plenty of room for a 'madman' to toss the contents over and over until they are thoroughly 'fatigued.' The final result will be neither a neat nor 'esthetic' arrangement, but it will taste good.

There is plenty of scope for imagination and originality, too, in the combination of ingredients, and especially in the choice of herbs used in the dressing. The following list by no means exhausts the endless possibilities open to anyone interested in the art of salad-making.

Vegetable salads are often served as hors d'oeuvres, and the recipes will also be found in Chapter X.

GENERAL RULES FOR MIXING SALADS

1. A large bowl and a long-handled fork and spoon, preferably wooden.

2. The best French or Italian olive oil (no substitutes).

3. White- or red-wine vinegar, plain or flavored with herbs, as preferred, but the herb vinegars are an improvement over most green or vegetable salads.

4. A pepper mill (the French are the best) — pepper should always be ground fresh.

5. Salt, mustard, a clove of garlic.

6. Herbs — fresh if possible.

7. A small pair of scissors to cut them.

If the dried herbs are used, they should be soaked first in the vinegar to be used in the dressing. It is highly desirable to dress the salad either at the table or shortly before serving. Exceptions: cooked vegetables, such as string beans, beets, or potatoes, which are better marinated for about an hour, and, of course, anything dressed with mayonnaise or sour cream.

The classic French dressing consists of:

One part vinegar to three and one-half or four parts oil.
Salt and pepper.
(The proportion of vinegar may be varied slightly, as some vegetables, like beets, require a trifle more.)

The bowl may first be rubbed with garlic; then put in the lettuce, mixed greens, vegetables, etc., which have been carefully dried with a towel; add the herbs, chives, chervil, etc., finely cut, then sprinkle with 1 Tbs. oil, turning over and over so as to coat the leaves well. Put the salt and freshly ground pepper in the salad spoon and add the vinegar, stirring well in the spoon; add a little oil and mix; then pour onto the salad slowly; add the rest of the oil and turn over and over until thoroughly incorporated.

Another method is to mix the dressing in a small dish or bowl, beating well with a small piece of ice, then pouring over the salad. Either method is equally satisfactory provided everything is thoroughly mixed at the end.

If the salad is to be served with the meat course it should be one of mixed greens; if a separate course, with crackers and cheese, it may be a more elaborate combination of vegetables, cooked or raw. The herbs most used in mixing a salad are chives, chervil, burnet, tarragon, basil, summer savory, and garden cress, but the list may be indefinitely extended according to taste and the materials at hand.

VARIOUS SALAD DRESSINGS

French dressing, with a little mustard added.
French dressing, with a little crumbled Roquefort cheese.

Sour Cream Dressings

1. 1 cup sour cream, beaten with 1 Tbs. lemon juice or vinegar, seasoned with paprika and celery salt, chopped chives.
2. 1 cup sour cream, salt, 1 Tbs. fresh tomato juice, and 1 tsp. lemon juice, beaten together.
3. 1 cup sour cream, ½ tsp. dry mustard, ½ tsp. salt, 2 Tbs. sugar, 3 egg yolks, and ¼ cup vinegar. Mix mustard, salt and sugar. Add to egg yolks and beat lightly. Stir in sour cream and vinegar. Cook in top of double boiler over hot water until mixture coats spoon. Chill before using.

Mayonnaise dressing: for cooked vegetables, it should be thinned with cream.

Russian Dressing

½ cup mayonnaise	1 tsp. minced green pepper
¼ cup chili sauce	1 tsp. minced chives
1 tsp. minced pimento	

Mix well and chill.

Sauce Vinaigrette

2 shallots, minced	1 Tbs. capers
2 small pickles, minced	¼ tsp. salt
2 sprigs parsley, minced	⅛ tsp. pepper
2 sprigs chervil, minced	2 Tbs. tarragon vinegar
2 sprigs tarragon, minced	4 Tbs. olive oil
½ tsp. minced chives	1 egg yolk, hard boiled

Mix together well, mashing the egg yolk with a fork. Serve with cold asparagus, artichokes, etc.

SALADS

ARTICHOKE

Served whole with French or mayonnaise dressing.

Hearts: alone or in mixture with beans, avocados, or zucchini.

Bottoms: with sauce vinaigrette.

ASPARAGUS

Fresh green asparagus may be cut up and combined with lettuce, French dressing, and chives, or served whole and French dressing passed. Cook with plenty of salt in boiling water and chill.

AVOCADO

Use only when soft. Do *not* slice or chill,[1] but scoop out of shell with teaspoon. Dress with olive oil, tarragon vinegar (or a little lime juice), salt, black pepper, and chives.

Combine with:

   (*a*) Tomatoes, quartered and treated with paprika, etc.

   (*b*) Grapefruit.

[1] Chilling tends to destroy the flavor.

(*c*) String beans, artichoke hearts, asparagus tips and sliced zucchini, *or* serve simply with salt and fresh lime or lemon juice.

'Guacamole' (*Mexican*)

Mash *very* ripe avocado with fork, add pulp of one tomato cut up (leave out seeds and juice if watery), a very little grated white onion, and small green chili pepper (canned), cut up, if available, otherwise a discreet amount of Tabasco. Add salt to taste, lemon or lime juice, and a little olive oil. Serve on lettuce leaves on a flat dish.

BEANS, STRING

Must be young and fresh; cut fine and cooked in salted boiling water, then chilled. Dress with oil, tarragon vinegar, salt, black pepper, and chopped chives or a little onion finely minced or grated.

Or, with sour cream dressing, chives, and summer savory.

Other Combinations

Mix with sliced artichoke hearts (canned or fresh); very ripe avocado and lettuce cut up and shredded, a few sliced zucchinis — asparagus tips (fresh) may also be added — a delicious combination.

Dressing: oil, tarragon vinegar, salt, pepper, chives.

String beans, young beets, and green peas, with mayonnaise.

BEETS

Cooked and hollowed out, filled with young peas mixed with mayonnaise and a little mint, if liked.

Chopped, with French dressing, celery seed, and caraway.

With watercress and chervil.

BROCCOLI

Boiled, chilled, and dressed with oil and vinegar.

CABBAGE

Shredded, with cut-up celery, and/or radishes, chives, French dressing.

Shredded, with grated or shredded carrot; French dressing or sour cream, mayonnaise thinned with cream, or mayonnaise with chopped tarragon.

CELERIAC

Boiled, sliced, and dressed with oil and vinegar. A little pimento is good with this.

CELERY

Cut up with apple, mayonnaise or French dressing.
Cut up with cabbage.

CHICORY (OR ENDIVE)

Rub bowl with garlic. French dressing with chopped hard-boiled egg is good.

CORN SALAD ('LAMB'S LETTUCE'; FRENCH, 'MÂCHE')

With French dressing, alone or in combination with other greens.

CUCUMBERS

(a) Slice thin, sprinkle with salt, and let stand about an hour. Combine with plain lettuce and dill; watercress or garden cress and chives; or any mixture of greens; also with tomatoes, quartered, and dressed with oil, vinegar, and pepper.

(*b*) Sliced thin, salted, etc., served with sour cream and chopped chives or dill or/and burnet.

ENDIVE, FRENCH

With French dressing, alone or in combination with other greens.

FINOCCHIO

Either raw or boiled and sliced. Add minced green tops of fennel to dressing.

FRUITS

Apple: sliced and mixed with lettuce, French dressing.

Apple and Celery: mayonnaise thinned with cream or French dressing.

Grapefruit and Lettuce: French dressing (less vinegar than usual, or use lemon juice), paprika.

Orange and Romaine: French dressing, paprika. (Good with duck.)

Pear: rather soft ripe Bartletts, Comice, or Anjou are best, sliced thin; lettuce, paprika, oil, and white-wine vinegar or lemon, a little salt.

Persimmon: French dressing and lettuce.

JERUSALEM ARTICHOKES

Boil (in their skins) in salted water with a few drops of lemon juice. Chill, peel, and slice; dress with chives, chervil, and French dressing or mayonnaise.

LEEKS

Boiled, cut in short lengths, and served with French dressing.

MIXED GREEN SALAD

Lettuce, watercress or curly cress, radishes cut up, young green leaves of corn salad or anything available, chives and chervil. (Combinations are unlimited in spring.)

'Vichy': a mixture of lettuce, watercress, escarole, chicory, dressed with red-wine vinegar, olive oil, mustard and garlic rubbed in the bowl, and fine herbs.

PARSNIP

Cooked until tender in salted boiling water. Chilled and cut up. French dressing.

POTATO SALAD

With dill or a few caraway seeds. The potatoes should be cut up and dressed while hot, with oil and vinegar, a little minced onion or chives, salt and pepper.

RUSSIAN SALAD

A mixture of cooked vegetables — string beans, peas, beets, carrots, potato, and a little onion, with mayonnaise; sometimes used as a hors d'oeuvre.

SPINACH SALAD

Pick out young fresh spinach, wash well, and leave the branches whole. Have a large kettle of boiling salted water ready and drop in a few branches at a time, cook 2 to 3 minutes, take out with a skimmer, hold under the cold water faucet for a moment, then lay on a wire rack, if possible, to drain. Chill thoroughly, arrange on a platter, and pass French dressing separately, made with fresh chopped chives and tarragon, or any salad herbs preferred.

SPRING SALAD

Young dandelion leaves, young sorrel, nasturtium, tar-ragon, burnet, upland cress, oil, vinegar, and chives.

TOMATOES

Peel, cut in quarters, sprinkle heavily with paprika and a little salt, and let stand covered in cool place (*not* in refrigerator) an hour or more before serving. Combine with any kind of lettuce, or mixture of several kinds, such as endive, romaine, etc. Bowl may be rubbed with garlic if liked. Add fresh or dried tarragon and basil, chives, and chervil, and dress with oil and tarragon vinegar, using smaller proportion than usual, as acid flavor of tomatoes is greater using this method.

With avocados: prepared as above, mixed with very ripe avocado.

Sliced: a French method. Cut in rather thick slices, sprinkle with salt and black pepper, a little minced onion or chives, and tarragon. Pour a few drops of olive oil on each slice and let stand in a cool place about an hour. Serve alone or on a bed of green mixed salad dressed with oil and vinegar.

Tomato jelly ring: filled with mixed vegetables, with French dressing or mayonnaise, or peas, or beans marinated with oil and vinegar.

Recipe for Tomato Jelly

1 large can tomatoes	2 peppercorns
½ medium-sized onion, sliced	2 Tbs. gelatine, soaked in
1 bay leaf	½ cup cold water
2 or 3 sprigs basil	Salt

Cook the tomatoes, onion, and herbs together about 20 minutes; add salt and strain. Add the gelatine and strain again into a ring mold or small cups.

VEGETABLE SALAD

Any combination of cooked or raw vegetables with French dressing or mayonnaise.

WATERCRESS

Alone or mixed with other greens.

Lettuce, beets, chervil and chives, oil, tarragon vinegar, salt, and black pepper.

Mixed with sections of orange. Serve with duck.

ZUCCHINI (ITALIAN SQUASH)

Boil whole without peeling; chill, cut in not too thin slices. Combine with lettuce, chives, marjoram and French dressing.

Excellent also mixed with string beans, artichokes, etc.

CHAPTER X

HORS D'OEUVRES, CHEESE, CHEESE ENTRÉES

LIST OF RECIPES

HORS D'OEUVRES

FONDS D'ARTICHAUTS VINAIGRETTE

Cold artichoke bottoms with sauce vinaigrette.

HEARTS OF ARTICHOKES
(*in oil*)

These come in cans and may have minced garlic, chives, salt, and lime or lemon juice added.

CHOPPED BEETS

Marinated with French dressing, minced chives and chervil, and served without lettuce.

CHICKEN LIVER PATÉ

Put chicken livers in small saucepan; set in water (or double boiler) and steam 10 minutes. Mash with a fork and add — for 4 livers — ½ clove garlic, crushed, 1 Tbs. sweet butter, a little salt, and 1 Tbs. brandy. Work all well together and add, if available, 2 truffles, minced fine. This should be kept in a small covered jar in refrigerator.

CHICKEN LIVER RELISH

Cook 3 chicken livers about 15 minutes in a small quantity of water, then chop fine with 3 hard-boiled eggs and mix thoroughly. Melt 4 Tbs. butter. In it fry 1 medium-sized onion finely cut, to a light brown. Throw liver-egg mixture into pan; add 2 Tbs. milk; salt and pepper to taste and mix well. Cook slowly 5 minutes. Put mixture into mold and allow to cool. Serve cold.

COLE SLAW

Shredded cabbage with grated or shredded carrot and a little minced celery or celery leaves and chives; French dressing or sour cream, mayonnaise thinned with cream, or mayonnaise with chopped tarragon.

CRABMEAT
(*with Russian dressing*)

Cold crabmeat served with a bowl of Russian dressing (Crab Louis).

Russian dressing: see page 150.

CUCUMBERS

Slice very thin; sprinkle with salt and let stand about an hour. They may then be dressed with oil and vinegar, black pepper, chopped chives, dill or burnet, or with sour cream and chopped chives.

'GUACAMOLE' (MEXICAN)

Mash a very ripe avocado with fork; add pulp of 1 tomato cut up (squeeze out seeds and juice if watery), ¼ tsp. grated white onion, and 1 small green chili pepper (canned) cut up, or a tiny amount of Tabasco and cayenne. Add salt to taste, lemon or lime juice, and a little olive oil. Mix thoroughly and arrange each portion on a lettuce leaf. Serve with toasted crackers.

HAM OR DRIED BEEF ROLLS

Mix cream cheese with a little prepared mustard and spread on very thin slices of boiled ham or dried beef. Roll up each slice and cut into 1½-in. lengths, spearing each with a toothpick.

OLIVES

Stuffed with pimentos, chilis, or onion.

Ripe olives may be marinated in a mixture of olive oil, a clove of garlic, crushed, salt, and a little vinegar or lemon juice. Keep in a covered jar in a cool place until needed.

POTATO SALAD

Use new potatoes; boil in their skins; peel and cut up while hot. Add a little minced onion, and dress with oil and vinegar, salt and black pepper. Mix thoroughly. Chopped chives may then be added and a few caraway seeds, or the finely chopped tops of dill sprinkled freely over the top.

RUSSIAN SALAD

½ cup diced cooked carrots	A little celery, minced **fine**
½ cup diced cooked potatoes	½ tsp. minced onion
¼ cup diced cooked beets	Minced chives
¼ cup cooked peas	Minced tarragon
¼ cup cooked string beans, cut into small pieces	Salt Pepper

First marinate with a French dressing, season and add mayonnaise thinned with a very little cream. Mix thoroughly, adding the minced herbs at the last.

SHRIMP (MAYONNAISE VERT)

Shrimps served with toothpicks and a bowl of green mayonnaise.

STUFFED EGGS
(with fine herbs)

6 hard-boiled eggs	½ tsp. mustard
Mayonnaise	1 tsp. minced chives
Salt	1 Tbs. minced tarragon,
•Pepper	thyme, or basil

Cut the eggs in half lengthwise; take out yolks, mash with a little mayonnaise, mustard, salt, pepper, and herbs. Fill the egg whites with this mixture; top with mayonnaise and sprinkle with minced herbs.

SLICED TOMATOES

Peel and cut tomatoes into thin slices. Arrange on a flat serving-dish. Sprinkle over each slice a little salt, pepper, minced chives, and tarragon. Then pour over a little olive oil and keep cold until ready to serve.

CHEESE

BOHEMIAN CHEESE SPREAD

2 Tbs. sweet butter   Worcestershire sauce
2 Tbs. Roquefort cheese   Cayenne pepper

Melt butter and cheese in double boiler, stirring until creamy. Add a few grains Cayenne and a little Worcestershire sauce. Stir well and serve on toasted crackers.

COTTAGE CHEESE

Mix with sour cream and minced chives. Spread on crackers or toasted rye bread.

With Sage

1 cup cottage cheese   ½ tsp. onion, minced
2 Tbs. fresh sage   1 Tbs. milk
2 Tbs. spinach leaves   Salt
1 tsp. chives, minced

Rub sage and spinach to a paste, adding a little milk. Press through sieve and stir the juice in the cheese with the onion, chives and salt to taste.

With Caraway

1 cup cottage cheese   1 tsp. caraway seeds
  (or cream cheese)   ¼ tsp. chives
Cream   ½ clove garlic, minced
½ tsp. salt   Few grains cayenne pepper

Mix the cheese to a smooth paste with cream; then add chives, garlic, caraway seeds, salt and pepper. Mix well and shape into a cake.

With Other Combinations

Coriander seeds
Basil and fennel
Chervil and chives
Rue, dill, and parsley.

CREAM OR COTTAGE CHEESE
(with fine herbs; for sandwiches)

Soften the cheese with a little cream; add a pinch of salt and any combinations of fine herbs, cut up very fine. This is especially good spread on thin slices of rye bread with caraway, and improves by keeping overnight in icebox.

EAST INDIA CURRY SPREAD
(for sandwiches and crackers)

2 oz. strong cheese, grated	Salt
2 Tbs. butter	Cayenne pepper
2 tsp. curry powder	1 Tbs. onion juice (optional)
2 eggs	

Melt butter in saucepan. When hot stir in curry powder and fry lightly. Add cheese, salt, pepper, etc. Lastly, stir in the eggs, which have been slightly beaten, and cook until it reaches the consistency of scrambled eggs. Allow to get cold before filling sandwiches.

SACHER CHEESE

1 lb. cottage cheese	1 Tbs. minced chives
2 egg yolks	1 tsp. olive oil
2 tsp. anchovy paste	1 tsp. dry mustard
1 Tbs. softened butter	1 tsp. minced parsley

Mix all ingredients and beat well. Force through strainer and heap in cone shape on large serving plate. Sprinkle with paprika and surround with small rolled anchovies, gherkins, sections of hard-boiled eggs, radishes, and celery. Chill until ready to use and serve with crackers.

SAVORY CHEESE ROLL

Mix cream cheese with a little cream and minced fine herbs — chives, chervil, parsley, tarragon, and thyme, or basil, or rosemary. Trim crusts from thin slices of rather soft sandwich bread, spread with mixture, roll and toast under broiler. The rolls should be finger size. These are very good served with tomato cocktail.

SAVORY CHEESE SPREAD

Rub bowl with garlic. Mix equal parts of cream cheese and Roquefort or Gorgonzola with a little olive oil and sherry. Cover and keep in the refrigerator. Add a little sherry occasionally if it is kept for any length of time.

SANDWICH FILLINGS AND SPREADS

Any of the above *herb* and *cream cheese mixtures* may be used for rye or whole-wheat bread sandwiches.

East India spread is excellent for small sandwiches, the bread cut very thin.

Chopped hard-boiled egg, mixed with mayonnaise and minced herbs.

Watercress: chop and marinate with a very little French or mayonnaise dressing; or mix with sweet butter and a little salt and spread on 'open' sandwiches (trim crusts) or butter thin slices of bread (on the loaf) spread with a mixture of egg yolk and a little mustard. Lay a sprig of watercress on the slice and roll up with the green dressing.

Curly cress: may be chopped and mixed with the butter before spreading.

Young mustard leaves are also good in sandwiches alone or mixed with curly cress.

CHEESE ENTRÉES

CHEESE FONDUE

Take as many eggs as there are guests, about a third as much by weight of Gruyère cheese, cut up fine or grated, and one-sixth of the weight of the eggs in butter. Beat the eggs well in a saucepan; add butter and cheese; place on fire and stir with a wooden spoon till thick and soft. Add salt according to age of the cheese and a strong dose of pepper (cayenne or black). Serve in a hot dish. (Six eggs = 1 lb.) (Brillat-Savarin.)

CHEESE TIMBALES

4 eggs	2 Tbs. finely grated Swiss cheese
1 cup milk	1 Tbs. finely grated Parmesan cheese
2½ Tbs. melted butter	½ tsp. salt
1 tsp. minced chives	⅛ tsp. pepper
1 tsp. basil	A few grains cayenne

Beat eggs slightly; add milk and other ingredients. Turn into buttered timbale molds, cover with heavy wax paper; set in pan of hot water and bake in a slow oven. Turn out on plate and pour over tomato cream sauce, flavored with basil.

TOMATO RABBIT OR 'CHILÉLY'

½ cup strong American cheese	4 large tomatoes (or 1 can)
2 Tbs. butter	2 white onions
1 tsp. prepared mustard	½ green pepper, seeds removed
(or ½ tsp. Colman's)	Dash Tabasco sauce
2 Tbs. cream	Dash cayenne pepper
½ tsp. Worcestershire sauce	

Grate or chop the cheese; rub to a paste with the butter, mustard, cream, Tabasco and Worcestershire sauce in the chafing-dish, and add pepper. Stir over hot water until melted and smooth. Then stir in quickly the following

sauce, which has been made in another saucepan, preferably an hour or two ahead of time.

Scald and skin the tomatoes, cut in small pieces, and add
the onion and pepper finely chopped. Cook over a hot fire
at least 30 minutes. If there is much tomato juice, pour
away some of it, as it should not be watery. After it has
been added to the cheese, stir until thoroughly mixed, and
serve on pilot wafers, with beer or ale.

RABBIT MEPHISTO

1 large tomato	¼ tsp. cayenne pepper
2 Tbs. butter	2 Tbs. catsup
½ lb. American cheese, grated	¼ cup beer
¼ tsp. English mustard	1 egg, beaten
	Toast

Slice tomato into four thick slices. Melt 1 Tbs. butter in
a chafing-dish; sauté slices directly over flame. Remove
slices to a warm plate. Fill lower part of chafing-dish with
hot water. Add remaining butter to chafing-dish and then
cheese. Place over hot water and cook until cheese melts.
Add seasoning and beer. When smooth and creamy, stir in egg.
Place tomato slices on toast and pour cheese mixture over.

SAVORY CHEESE RING

4 Tbs. butter	2 Tbs. chopped green peppers
5 Tbs. flour	1 Tbs. minced onion
2 cups milk	¼ tsp. Gulden's mustard
½ tsp. salt	3 egg yolks
½ cup grated American cheese	3 egg whites, beaten
⅓ cup diced Swiss cheese	¼ tsp. paprika
3 Tbs. chopped celery	

Melt butter and add flour. When blended, add milk and
cook until creamy sauce forms. Add cheeses and seasonings and cook one minute, stirring constantly. Beat well,
add rest of ingredients, mixing lightly. Pour into buttered
ring or round mold. Set in pan of hot water and bake 35
minutes in moderately slow oven. Unmold carefully and
fill center with creamed celery.

CHAPTER XI

BEVERAGES

LIST OF RECIPES

Herbs have always been used in the making of beverages, and the art of brewing and distilling was an essential part of the education of the medieval housewife. As she was also the family doctor, she learned to use simples — or medicinal herbs — and almost all herbs were believed to have medicinal values. The tisanes or herb teas have always been popular remedies, and in Europe physicians still prescribe them, especially camomile. There are fewer varieties of tea herbs available in our American gardens, though one may now buy imported ones, such as lime blossom, quatres fleurs, or herb maté.

HERB TEAS OR TISANES

A general rule for making herb teas is as follows:
One teaspoon dried leaves or flowers to one cup of boiling water; let steep 5 minutes and serve plain or with a slice of lemon. It may be sweetened with honey or sugar. If the fresh herb is used, double the quantity.

RECIPES

ANISE TEA

Make according to the above rule.

BALM TEA

2 tsp. sugar	Juice of ½ lemon
6 cloves	12 sprigs lemon balm

Put lemon balm, sugar, cloves, and lemon juice into a jug. Pour 1 pt. of boiling water over them. Leave them to steep and cover jug. When cool, strain. May be served hot or cold.

CAMOMILE TEA

The dried blossoms only are used for this.

PEPPERMINT TEA

Made with the fresh leaves, this is especially good.

ROSEMARY TEA

Best made with the fresh rosemary when in bloom.

SAGE AND WORMWOOD TEAS

These are purely medicinal.

MINT TEA
(as made in Morocco)

The host puts into the teapot green tea, a large amount of sugar, a handful of fresh mint, and pours boiling water over the mixture.

This is served in small glasses. To be polite, one should drink three glasses. (Eleanor Hoffmann.)

HERB AND FRUIT PUNCHES

BOWLS — PEACH

6 large peaches, cut up
2 crushed pits
Sugar to taste
1 Tbs. kirsch

1 bottle light dry white wine (Alsatian or New York State)
½ bottle champagne (California)
Orange mint
Lemon balm

Put cut-up peaches in punchbowl with crushed pits, sprinkle with sugar and kirsch. Crush a little, then pour over wine and let stand at least an hour. Add large piece of ice, mint, balm, and lastly champagne, well chilled.

BOWLS — PINEAPPLE

1 ripe pineapple, shredded
Sugar to taste
2 Tbs. brandy

1 bottle dry Moselle or Alsatian wine
½ bottle champagne (California)
Spearmint

Put shredded pineapple in punchbowl, sprinkle with

sugar and brandy. Crush a little, then pour over wine and let stand at least an hour. Add large piece of ice, spearmint, and lastly champagne, well chilled.

WOODRUFF — 'MAI BOWLE'

1 orange, sliced with rind left on	Handful woodruff blossoms and leaves
1 Tbs. sugar	
1 qt. Rhine wine or Moselle	1 pt. champagne

Put woodruff blossoms and leaves into a punchbowl. Add orange and sugar. Pour in Rhine wine or Moselle and let stand about two hours. Add a chunk of ice and the champagne just before serving. Wild strawberries may be added to this bowl and give a delicious flavor.

CIDER CUP

¼ lb. lump sugar, rubbed well with lemon rind	Juice of 1½ lemons
	3 wineglassfuls sherry
1 qt. cider (English bottled if possible)	½ nutmeg, grated
	Borage

Add the cider to sugar, lemon rind, and juice, with a handful of borage. Let stand an hour; chill, add sherry and nutmeg.

CIDER — MULLED

1½ qts. cider	1 wineglassful whiskey or applejack
3 oranges, stuck with cloves	5 or 6 lumps sugar, rubbed with lemon peel

Boil together the cider, sugar, and oranges for 3 or 4 minutes. Add whiskey or applejack and pour into a punchbowl, letting the oranges float about. Serve hot.

CLARET CUP

1 bottle claret
1 pt. seltzer or soda water
A small bunch balm
A small bunch borage
1 orange, sliced

1 lemon, sliced
Rind of ½ cucumber, sliced thick
1 Tbs. cognac
1 oz. rock candy, or coarse sugar

Put all ingredients except soda water in a punchbowl, cover and let stand an hour. Stir well and add large piece of ice and the soda.

GRAPEJUICE PUNCH

1 qt. grapejuice
4 lemons
1 cup sugar

Stick cinnamon
Borage
Mint

Squeeze the lemon juice into a jug, add a handful of borage and the sugar. Let stand an hour, then add the grapejuice and 1 qt. of ice water (or seltzer). Pour over a large lump of ice into the punchbowl and garnish with mint.

HERB PUNCH

1 large handful lemon balm
2 large handfuls borage
1 large handful mint
Sugar syrup (1 cup sugar and
    ½ cup water)
3 qts. Canada Dry ginger ale

1 qt. strong tea
Juice of 6 lemons
Juice of 2 oranges
1 cup pineapple, or any other
    fruit juice

Pour 1½ qts. boiling water over balm leaves and let steep 20 minutes. Strain onto borage and mint in a large bowl, add fruit juices, tea, and syrup. Let stand overnight or at least six hours. Strain, add a large piece of ice, the ginger ale, and a fresh bunch of mint.

FRESH MINT PUNCH

Crush 12 sprigs mint, squeeze the juice of 6 oranges and 3 lemons over them, and add ¾ cup sugar. Stir well and then put a lump of ice in the punchbowl, pour mixture over; add 1 pt. cider and 3 pts. ginger ale.

MINT JULEP — A SOUTHERN RECIPE

Into each tall glass, put 2 or 3 sprigs of spearmint, 1 scant tsp. sugar, and half a jigger of cold water. Bruise the mint and stir until the sugar is dissolved. Add a jigger and a half (or more) of Bourbon whiskey, then fill the glass full of ice crushed as finely as possible. Beat with a long-handled spoon until glass is well frosted, adding more ice if necessary, and serve with a large sprig of mint in each glass.

RASPBERRY AND RHUBARB CUP

Cut up a pound of red rhubarb and boil it in a quart of water with 2 slices of lemon for 20 minutes; then strain it and add 4 oz. of sugar, 2 Tbs. raspberry vinegar, and serve chilled with grated nutmeg, crushed borage leaves, and mint.

RASPBERRY VINEGAR

8 qts. raspberries
1 qt. cider vinegar
Sugar

Pour vinegar over 4 qts. raspberries in a large bowl or crock and let stand 24 hours. Strain onto 2 more qts. of berries; let stand another 24 hours, and strain onto 2 more qts. of berries. The following day strain through a jelly bag; measure and add sugar — cup for cup. Stir well and boil 10 minutes. Skim and bottle. Cork tightly.

Use about 2 Tbs. of the syrup to a large glass of ice water, stir well, and serve in hot weather. A sprig of mint in each glass is a pleasant addition.

SANTA BARBARA FRUIT PUNCH

1 qt. strong tea	Mint
Juice of 12 lemons	4 bottles C. & C. ginger ale
Juice of 12 oranges	1 qt. sparkling cider (or apple juice)
Cucumber rind	Sweeten with 'Five Fruits'

Add about 1 qt. fresh strawberries or any other fruit in season.

TEA PUNCH

1 qt. tea (India)	Sugar to taste (about 1 Tbs.)
1 pt. bottle White Rock or soda	Borage and lemon balm
Rind of lemon, cut very thin	Wineglass of curaçao

Crush lemon rind, borage, and balm with sugar and curaçao. Add hot tea and let stand about an hour. Add ice and soda and serve in punchbowl.

COCKTAILS

ABSINTHE

2 parts pineapple juice	Juice of 1 lime
1 part rum (Santa Cruz or Puerto Rico)	2 sprigs wormwood

Shake well with crushed ice and 1 leaf wormwood. Add another sprig of wormwood slightly bruised, in each glass.

CRANBERRY

1 qt. cranberries
2 qts. boiling water
2 cups sugar

Boil until berries are soft, rub through strainer. Add a bouquet of fresh herbs, lemon balm, lemon thyme, burnet, hyssop, and rue — a sprig only of the last two; simmer for 5 minutes; strain and bottle.

The canned juice may be used, brought to a boil, and the herbs added as above. English apple mint or curly mint give excellent flavor and may be used alone. (Mrs. Webster.)

RUM COCKTAIL OR COOLER

1 jigger rum (any kind)	White Rock or soda
Juice of 1 green lime	1 sprig mint
2 tsp. sugar	

Put in tall glass, squeezing lime and adding ½ rind. Fill up with soda and cracked ice, stir well and serve, garnished with more mint.

TOMATO COCKTAIL

1 qt. pure tomato juice	The leaves of a head of celery
(canned or fresh)	(or lovage)
1 onion, sliced	A handful of basil
½ tsp. salt	

Boil together 10 minutes, strain and bottle or serve in pitcher well chilled. Add a few tarragon leaves and serve with a quarter of lemon or lime to each person.

VERMOUTH COCKTAIL OR COOLER

1 jigger cinzano (sweet)	1 sprig fresh wormwood
1 jigger cinzano (dry) (or French)	1 sprig fresh lemon balm (or
1 squeeze lemon juice	lemon thyme)
1 twisted piece of lemon peel	Seltzer or White Rock to fill glass

Put all ingredients in tall glass, add cracked ice and stir well.

WINES

DANDELION

Pick the heads only of the dandelions; spread them out on sheets of paper to get rid of insects. To each gallon of flower heads, add 1 gallon of water, 2 oranges, 1 lemon. 1 oz. root ginger (crushed). Tie the ginger in a muslin bag. Put into a pan and bring it all to the boil, and boil it for 20 minutes. Then strain it and add 4 lbs. sugar. If not clear, add the white of an egg, and to make it work, put in ½ oz. yeast on a slice of bread. Leave it a week, strain and bottle it loosely at first, then tighter.

It should stand for 6 months before using. (Leyel.)

ELDERBERRY

Gather the berries on a dry day, clean from the stalks and put them into an earthenware pan. Pour 2 gals. boiling water to every 3 gals. of berries. Press the berries into the water. Cover them closely and leave them till the next day. Then strain the juice from the fruit through a sieve, and when this is done, squeeze from the berries any remaining juice.

Measure the juice and add to every gallon 3 lbs. sugar, 6 cloves, and 1 Tbs. ginger. Boil it for 20 minutes, removing the scum as it rises. Put it when cool into a well-washed and dry cask. Entirely fill the cask, and pour very gently into the bung-hole a large spoonful of new yeast, mixed with a very small quantity of the wine. Have at least a quart of extra juice in reserve in order to fill up the cask as the wine evaporates. This improves with age. Excellent mulled.

ELDERBLOW

3 lbs. raisins	9 lbs. sugar
1 qt. elder flower blossoms	2 tsp. lemon juice
3 gals. water	1 yeast cake

Boil water and sugar together. Pour over blossoms. When cool, add lemon juice and yeast. Put in a crock and let stand 9 days. Strain through cheesecloth, add raisins and put back in jar. Bottle 6 months later. A good addition to sliced fruit.

LEMON BALM

4 gals. water	4 egg whites, well beaten
8 lbs. loaf sugar	1 peck balm leaves
Juice of 6 lemons	Slice of toast spread with yeast

Boil together the water, sugar, lemon juice, and egg whites for 45 minutes, skimming well. Then take the balm leaves, put them in a tub with the thin peeling of the lemons; pour the boiling liquor on, stirring well until almost cold. Put on top the toast spread with yeast. Let it work for 2 or 3 days, then strain off, squeezing the leaves through a cloth and afterward through a flannel bag into a cask. Stop lightly until it has done hissing, then bung down close. At the end of 3 months, bottle. (Mrs. M. E. Moulam, Derbyshire.)

ROSEMARY

Chop sprigs of green rosemary, pour over them any white wine and let stand a week. Strain and bottle.

LIQUEURS AND CORDIALS

A BASIC RECIPE FOR MAKING LIQUEURS

The leaves or the fruits are steeped in brandy or alcohol for a period varying with each recipe. A syrup of sugar and water (2 cups sugar, 1 cup water) is made and added while still boiling hot. The liqueur is then filtered and bottled.

ANGELICA LIQUEUR

2 oz. of freshly gathered stems of angelica, chopped up and steeped in 2 pts. of good brandy during 5 days. Add 1 Tbs. skinned bitter almonds reduced to a pulp. Strain the liquid through fine muslin and add 1 pt. syrup made by boiling 2 cups sugar and 1 cup water for 5 minutes. Filter and bottle.

BLACK CHERRY BRANDY

Cherries sufficient to make 1 qt. juice	1½ cups sugar boiled to a syrup with ¾ cup water
1 qt. brandy	Stick of cinnamon

Crush and strain cherries and put juice, brandy, cinnamon, and about 20 crushed pits into a covered crock. Let stand 5 days. Add to hot syrup and filter into bottles.

MARIGOLD CORDIAL

1 peck marigold petals	4 Tbs. liquid yeast
1½ lbs. seeded raisins	1 oz. gelatine
7 lbs. sugar	1 lb. rock candy
2 lbs. honey	1 pt. brandy
3 gals. water	6 oranges
3 eggs	

Put the marigold petals into an earthenware bowl with the raisins. Pour over them a boiling liquid made of the sugar, honey, and water. Clear this liquid while it is boiling with the whites and shells of the eggs, and strain it before putting in the flowers. Cover up the bowl and leave for 48 hours. Stir it well and leave it for another 24 hours. Then strain it and put it into a 6-gal. cask, which has been well cleaned, and add to it the rock candy and the rinds of the oranges, which have been peeled and stripped of all white pith. Stir into it the liquid yeast and cover up the bung-hole. Leave it to work till it froths out; when the fermentation is over, pour in the brandy and the gelatine, which has been dissolved. Stop the cask and leave it for several months.

TARRAGON LIQUEUR

1 qt. brandy
A good handful leaves of tarragon

Leave 5 days (more will make it bitter). Syrup of 1½ cups sugar to each quart and only enough water to dissolve and make it boil. Just before bottling, add 2 ounces of orange flower water to each quart of liquor.

CHAPTER XII

FRUITS AND FRUIT DESSERTS

LIST OF RECIPES

COMBINATIONS OF FRESH FRUIT (Varieties)

COMPOTES OF FRESH FRUIT (Directions)

APPLES
Baked (stuffed with Quince, Raisins, Prunes, or with Honey)
Charlotte
Cider Applesauce
Cider Jelly
Compote
With Ginger
With Orange
With Prunes and Raisins
With Sherried Raisins
Glazed Mint
Minted
Scalloped
Spiced
Tapioca
Tart — Deep-Dish

APRICOTS
Baked (with Orange Rind)
Canned Halves soaked in Liqueur
Apricot Compote (with Curaçao)
Apricot and Pineapple Sago
Apricot Wine Jelly
Deep-Dish Tart

BLACKBERRIES
Creole Pudding
Flummery
Deep-Dish Tart
Shortcake

BLUEBERRIES
Betty
Pudding
Deep-Dish Tart
Stewed

CHERRIES
Bread Pudding
Compote of Black Cherries
With Apricots and Pineapple
Fresh Cherry Coupe
Deep-Dish Tart

CRANBERRIES
Relish

CURRANTS
With Red Raspberries
Sago (Rote Grütze)

DESSERTS
(To serve with Fruits)
Coeur à la Crème
Crème Brûlée
Crème à l'Amande

DESSERTS
Creamy Rice
Rice Mold
Ring of Rice
Custards (Honey, Maple, Marigold)
Ice Cream
Junket

ELDERBERRY
Deep-Dish Tart

FIGS
Compote
With Port Wine
With Shredded Orange Peel
Fresh Figs with Honey

FRUIT JELLIES
Mixed Fruit in Orange Jelly

FRUIT SAGO OR TAPIOCA
Basic Recipe
Crushed Fruit
Currant (Rote Grütze)
Rhubarb
Pineapple (Goula Malacca)
Raspberry
Strawberry

FRUITS (FRESH OR COOKED)
(To Serve with Rice, Custards, Cheese, etc.)
Red Raspberries
Strawberries
Preserved Quince
Cut-up Peaches
Brandied Peaches
Sherried Apricots, Peaches etc.

LEMON
Jelly
Ring Mold of Lemon Ice
Water Ice

LIME
Jelly
Water Ice

MELONS
Cantaloupe
Casaba   } See Fresh Fruits
Honeydew
Watermelon

MIXED FRUIT
Coupes
Méli-Mélo
(See also Cut-up Fresh Fruits)

MINT
Jelly (with Mixed Fruit)
Ice (with Fresh Fruit)

ORANGES
Cut up (mixed with other Fruits)
Jelly
Water Ice

PEACHES
Baked
With Brown Sugar
With Orange Rind
Compote
With Red Wine
With Kirsch
Cup
Flambée
Royal
Pudding
In Red Wine
In White Wine

PEARS
Baked
No. 1
No. 2
Compote
With Ginger

WATER ICES
  Lemon or Lime
  Mint
  Orange
  Pineapple

WATER ICES
  Red Raspberry
  Strawberry
  Tangerine

It has always been customary to finish a meal with fruit, and this custom has a sound basis in the correct planning of a healthful and attractive diet. If the meal is well balanced as to proteins, carbohydrates, and fats, with green vegetables for vitamins and minerals, then a hearty dessert is unnecessary and the perfect ending is fresh fruit, a compote, or a simple fruit dessert — not too sweet. As novelty and variety are important factors in the psychology of taste, the recipes which follow cover a wide range both as to varieties of fruits and ways to prepare and serve them.

Fresh fruit, like fresh vegetables, is a luxury, and we are fortunate in this country in having both in great variety and abundance. Fruits are worthy of careful preparation and more general use in place of heavier, richer food.

In serving fresh fruit the flavor will be much better if it is not chilled. This is contrary to the usual American custom, but if you have ever picked strawberries or raspberries warm from the sun and eaten them on the spot, you know how much more delicious they are than when served fresh from the Frigidaire or on a bed of ice. The same applies to tomatoes, which lose flavor when chilled.

COMBINATIONS OF FRESH FRUIT

GRAPEFRUIT

Cut in half, cut out center, and loosen the sections with a sharp knife. Sprinkle with sugar and a little chopped mint. Pour over 1 Tbs. sherry and let stand 1 hour or more before serving.

With Honey

Instead of sugar use 1 tsp. honey to each half grapefruit.

Mixed with Other Fruit

Cut up in small pieces and combine with orange or tangerine and pineapple. Sprinkle with sugar and maraschino, kirsch, or sherry to taste. Serve in individual dishes.

MELONS

Honeydew or Casaba melons may be cut in quarters or eighths and served with lemon or lime juice squeezed over them, and maraschino or kirsch to taste.

Watermelon may be cut in balls and a little sugar, lemon juice, and chopped mint added. Serve alone or mixed with other varieties of melons. This should stand an hour before serving.

PEACHES

May be cut up and allowed to stand with a little sugar and kirsch to taste. They may also be mixed with raspberries — with or without the liqueur.

PINEAPPLE

Shred or tear apart a pineapple with a silver fork. Sprinkle with sugar and a little liqueur if liked — maraschino or kirsch — and a few crushed mint leaves (remove before serving). Strawberries cut in halves may also be added.

RASPBERRIES

May be served with cut-up peaches as above, or alone with sugar and Bordeaux or claret (¼ cup to 1 qt. of fruit) poured over them and allowed to stand an hour, or sweetened with honey and a little liqueur added.

STRAWBERRIES

May be prepared the same way with either white wine or red.

COMPOTES OF FRESH FRUITS

Compotes are made with fresh fruit cooked quickly in a light syrup — 1 cup sugar to 1 cup water. If the fruit is very ripe, the hot syrup may be poured over it without further cooking.

For apples and pears: a piece of lemon rind and a stick of cinnamon, a few cloves, or ginger root may be cooked with the syrup. If the flavor of wine or liqueur is liked, it should be added after the syrup is cooked, or the fruit may be soaked in it first and the hot syrup then poured over.

Very ripe peaches are good scalded or steamed, the peel slipped off and hot raspberry syrup poured over without further cooking.

APPLES

BAKED APPLES STUFFED WITH QUINCE

Core the apples, stuff with bits of preserved quince, pour around some of the quince juice; cover and bake in slow oven.

Raisins or cooked prunes may be used instead of quince. Put about an inch of water in the casserole and cover while baking.

Honey may be used to fill the holes, instead of sugar; add also a small piece of orange rind to each apple, and a little orange juice to the water in the bottom of the pan.

APPLE CHARLOTTE

Cut bread into slices ¼ in. thick, then into strips 1½ in. wide, and as long as the height of the mold to be used; cut one piece to fit the top of mold, then divide it into 5 or 6 pieces. Butter mold, dip slices of bread into melted butter and maple syrup, and arrange them on the bottom and around sides of the mold, fitting closely together or overlapping. Fill the center full with applesauce made of tart apples stewed till tender, then broken into coarse pieces and seasoned with butter and sugar. Cover the top with bread and bake in a hot oven about a half hour. The bread should be amber colored like toast. Turn carefully onto a flat dish and serve with cream.

CIDER APPLESAUCE

Boil 2 qts. sweet cider until reduced to 1 qt. Add enough peeled cut-up apples to half fill kettle, a little cinnamon, and 1 cup brown sugar. Cook slowly until soft.

CIDER JELLY

2 Tbs. gelatine, dissolved in
½ cup cold water
2 cups sweet cider, boiling hot
¾ cup sugar
⅓ cup lemon juice
1 Tbs. applejack

Soak gelatine in cold water 5 minutes. Add remaining ingredients in order given. Pour in mold and chill. Serve with whipped cream slightly sweetened and flavored with a few drops of applejack, and sprinkled with nutmeg.

COMPOTE
(with ginger)

Make a syrup of 2 cups water, 2 cups sugar, and a piece of lemon peel. Cook halves or quarters in this until clear, add a little cut-up preserved ginger and ¼ cup ginger syrup, or cook 2 or 3 pieces of crushed green ginger root in the syrup before adding apples.

With Orange

Peel, core, and cut into slices firm, tart apples. Cover with orange juice — one orange to three apples; add sugar to taste and the rind of 2 oranges chopped very fine. Cook down until a thick sauce.

This is very good made with dried apples. Soak the apples overnight; allow the juice and rind of 4 oranges to 1 package of the dried apples, and cook slowly together with sugar to taste, until soft and mushy.

With Prunes and Raisins

Make a thin syrup of 1 cup sugar to 1 cup water, cooked with a piece of lemon peel. Add peeled and quartered apples; cook until they can be pierced easily with a fork; then add about 2 cooked prunes and 6 sultana raisins to each apple. Simmer 15 minutes and serve cold.

With Sherried Raisins

Cook muscatel raisins in sherry until they have absorbed all the liquid. Cook sliced apples in a thin sugar syrup with a slice of lemon peel, until clear. Cool and mix with the raisins.

GLAZED MINT APPLES

6 large apples	2 cups water
2 cups sugar	24 mint sprigs

Boil sugar and water together for 15 minutes. Pare and

core apples and place in a shallow saucepan. Pour the syrup over them; add 18 of the mint sprigs tied in a bunch and simmer slowly till the apples are clear. Turn often to prevent them from becoming mushy. Remove carefully, baste with the syrup, and put a sprig of mint in the hole of each apple. By the time they are done, the syrup should be ready to jell. If not, boil down rapidly and then pour over the apples. Serve hot or cold with roast lamb or pork, or with cream.

MINTED APPLES

1 cup water	¼ cup chopped mint
½ cup sugar	2 large apples

Boil the water, sugar, and mint 3 minutes; add a bit of green food color. Peel and quarter the apples and cook in syrup until tender. Strain syrup and pour over apples.

SCALLOPED APPLES

Pare, core, and slice apples as if for pie. Butter a pyrex pie dish, sprinkle with fine bread crumbs, and fill to the top with sliced apples. Sprinkle with brown sugar, a little cinnamon, and dabs of butter and cover lightly with bread crumbs. Bake in slow oven and serve warm.

SPICED APPLES

Select sweet apples, cut in halves without peeling; take out core and stick 3 cloves in each half. Lay in greased casserole, sprinkle with brown sugar, grated nutmeg, and a little lemon rind. Dot with butter and add a little water. Bake covered in hot oven a half hour.

APPLE TAPIOCA

½ cup Minute tapioca	6 tart apples
2½ cups boiling water	Butter
⅛ tsp. salt	Cinnamon or nutmeg
⅓ cup sugar	

Cook tapioca in boiling water with the salt, in a double boiler until transparent. Arrange the apples, pared and cored, in a buttered baking-dish; fill centers with sugar, a dab of butter, and nutmeg or cinnamon. Pour over the tapioca and bake in moderate oven till apples are soft. Serve warm.

APPLE TART — DEEP-DISH

Slice tart apples very thin and fill pyrex baking-dish to the top, add sugar to taste, a little cinnamon or nutmeg, and a little butter.

Cover with a simple piecrust, or very rich biscuit dough, and bake in a hot oven.

Serve cool, but not cold, with cream.

APRICOTS

BAKED
(with orange rind)

Place halves of canned apricots in pyrex pie dish or oval baking-dish. Grate orange rind over the apricots, add some of their syrup, and bake in oven or broil under gas flame. Add about 1 Tbs. curaçao and serve cold.

CANNED HALVES SOAKED IN LIQUEUR

The halves of canned apricots or peaches may be drained and soaked in brandy or any liqueur in a serving-dish. The syrup from the can should be boiled down, adding more sugar if liked, and poured over the fruit, then chilled before serving.

COMPOTE WITH CURAÇAO

Drain a pint of canned apricots and place on a compote dish. Put liquor in a saucepan and add 1 Tbs. sugar and the rind of an orange. Boil 10 minutes; remove rind and add 2 Tbs. curaçao; stir and pour over the apricots.

APRICOT AND PINEAPPLE SAGO

½ cup tapioca
¼ cup sugar
¼ tsp. salt
2 Tbs. lemon juice
1 cup apricot syrup

1½ cups pineapple juice
6 apricot halves, cut up
A few pieces shredded canned
  or fresh pineapple

Cook tapioca in double boiler with the fruit juice for a half hour; then add sugar and cook a half hour longer or until perfectly clear. Turn out in glass bowl, add fruit, and serve very cold with plain or whipped cream.

APRICOT WINE JELLY

¼ cup boiling water
½ cup tangerine or orange juice
½ cup apricot syrup
¼ cup sherry
2 Tbs. brandy or curaçao
1 Tbs. gelatine, dissolved in
3 Tbs. cold water

½ Tbs. lemon juice
¼ cup sugar
A pinch of salt
⅔ cup canned apricots, cut
  into pieces

Boil water and sugar one minute. Add sherry, apricot syrup, fruit juice, brandy, salt, and gelatine. Add the apricots to jelly mixture, and turn into mold. Chill thoroughly and serve with or without whipped cream. If not stiff enough to mold, serve in glasses topped with whipped cream.

DEEP-DISH TART

(See page 213)

BLACKBERRIES

CREOLE PUDDING

1 qt. blackberries	1 lb. loaf sponge cake, crumbled
1 cup butter	6 eggs
1½ cups powdered sugar	

Cook blackberries over low flame about 4 minutes. Cream butter until soft. Add powdered sugar gradually, beating until light and thick. Combine this with the fruit, then add sponge cake. Mix thoroughly. Beat egg yolks thoroughly and stir into mixture. Beat egg whites until stiff but not dry and fold in. Pour into a buttered baking-dish and bake in a moderately hot oven (375° F.) 30 to 40 minutes. Serve cold with whipped cream.

BLACKBERRY FLUMMERY

½ cup Minute tapioca	Lemon rind
1 cup blackberry juice	⅔ cup sugar
1 cup boiling water	3 cups blackberries

Cook tapioca in the blackberry juice and water, with lemon rind, until clear. Remove from fire, add sugar, and when cool stir in the fresh blackberries. Set aside until ice cold and serve in glasses with sweetened whipped cream.

DEEP-DISH TART

(See page 213)

SHORTCAKE

(See page 213)

BLUEBERRIES

BLUEBERRY BETTY

Butter slices of bread, enough to fill a pudding dish; trim crusts and cut into 4 pieces each. Butter the pudding dish well, arrange alternate layers of bread and blueberries, with sugar to taste, until the dish is full. Cover and bake in a moderate oven. Serve cold with cream.

BLUEBERRY MOLD

Cut slices of bread ½ in. thick; remove the crusts. Fit the slices closely together on the bottom and sides of a plain mold, leaving no spaces. Heat 1 qt. fresh blueberries with a cup of sugar until the juice runs freely. Stir until the sugar is dissolved and stew just long enough to soften the berries. Fill the mold to the top, cover with bread slices, and pack in bowl or pan of ice for several hours. Turn out on platter and serve with cream.

DEEP-DISH TART
(*See page* 213)

Stewed, plain or with pieces of bread.

CHERRIES

CHERRY BREAD PUDDING

Arrange alternate layers of stoned sour red cherries and bread crumbs in a buttered quart pudding dish. Season each layer with bits of butter, 1 Tbs. sugar, and a pinch of nutmeg. When the dish is filled, add a syrup made from 1 Tbs. water and 2 Tbs. sugar; cover the top with crumbs; place the dish in a pan of boiling water and cook for about an hour in a moderate oven.

COMPOTE OF BLACK CHERRIES

1 lb. cherries, pitted	A few of the pits, cracked
1 cup sugar, boiled to a	and crushed
syrup with	A piece of lemon rind
1 cup water	

Add cherries and crushed pits to syrup and stew gently about 10 minutes.

COMPOTE
(with apricots and pineapple)

Canned red cherries and canned apricot halves may be heated together and served hot with canned pineapple slices cut in quarters.

FRESH CHERRY COUPE

Stone 2 cups ripe sweet cherries, crack a few of the stones, and crush the kernels. Place with cherries and 4 Tbs. sugar in a bowl. Pour over 2 Tbs. kirsch and I Tbs. curaçao, and keep in refrigerator till needed. Serve in champagne glasses topped with lemon or orange ice.

DEEP-DISH TART
(See page 213)

CRANBERRIES

RELISH

1 qt. cranberries	1 orange
3 red apples	2 cups sugar (scant)

Wash cranberries well. Core the apples, remove seeds

from orange, but do not peel either. Put all through second meat grinder. Add sugar and mix well. Do not cook. Serve cold. Results better if served one or two days after making.

CURRANTS

WITH RED RASPBERRIES

Combine equal parts of currants and raspberries; sprinkle with sugar and let stand half an hour.

SAGO ('ROTE GRÜTZE')

3 cups currant juice	¼ lb. sago
1 to 1½ cups sugar	Small piece lemon peel,

Boil the sago slowly in a little water for a half hour in a double boiler. Add the currant juice, sugar, and lemon peel. Boil a half hour longer or until cooked. Pour into molds and cool.

This may be made with half raspberry and half currant juice, or all raspberry with lemon peel.

DESSERTS TO SERVE WITH FRUITS

COEUR À LA CRÈME

Mash 2 or 3 cakes of Philadelphia cream cheese with a fork, adding enough cream to make double the quantity. Mix thoroughly until perfectly smooth, adding a little salt. Dip a heart-shaped mold in ice-water and wipe dry. Half fill the mold with the cheese mixture and chill thoroughly. Turn out on a round platter and surround with sugared raspberries, or strawberries, or a mixture of both.

This may also be made with cottage cheese.

CRÈME BRÛLÉE

Beat yolks of 4 eggs. Boil 1 pt. cream one minute and pour over eggs, stirring well. Put on fire and let it come slowly to the boiling point. Pour into a baking-dish to cool. Sprinkle brown sugar over the top 15 minutes before serving and set in another dish of cracked ice. Then put under the broiler until sugar begins to melt and form a crust. Put in icebox to cool and serve with any cooked fruit.

CRÈME À L'AMANDE

Add a few drops of almond extract to the cream and egg mixture in the above recipe, and a few chopped almonds to the sugar before putting it under the broiler.

CREAMY RICE

⅓ cup rice	1 Tbs. sugar
2 to 3 cups milk	Cinnamon or nutmeg
¼ tsp. salt	

Wash rice well and cook in double boiler until soft or about 1½ hours, stirring occasionally. Add a little more milk if necessary, as it should be creamy and not stiff when cold. Pour into a bowl or shallow dish and sprinkle with a little cinnamon or nutmeg. Serve as an accompaniment to fresh or cooked fruit.

RICE MOLD

3 cups milk	1 Tbs. gelatine, dissolved in a
A little grated lemon rind	little hot water
⅓ cup rice	1 cup whipped cream, sweetened
1 egg white	A few drops lemon juice
1 saltspoon salt	½ cup sugar

Put milk and the grated lemon rind in a double boiler

When this boils, add rice and salt and cook until the rice is tender and the milk nearly boiled away. Stir in stiffly beaten egg white, sugar, and gelatine. Allow the mixture to cool, but before it stiffens fold in the whipped cream and lemon juice. Pour immediately into a ring mold and place in the refrigerator to become firm. Serve unmolded with the center filled with fresh or cooked fruits.

RING OF RICE FILLED WITH COOKED FRUITS

Cook rice in milk and put in ring mold. When cold, unmold and fill center with any cooked or preserved fruit, pouring some of the syrup around, or passing it separately.

OTHER DESSERTS WITH WHICH FRESH OR COOKED FRUITS MAY BE SERVED

Custards

Plain or made with honey (see page 233) or maple syrup.
Marigold custard: Add crushed marigold (calendula) petals to plain baked or soft custard. The latter can be used as a pudding sauce.
Ice cream: See page 213.

ELDERBERRIES

DEEP-DISH TART

1 cup sugar	1 Tbs. flour
3 cups elderberries	1 Tbs. butter
2 cups blackberries	Salt

Make a simple piecrust or very rich biscuit dough. Fill pyrex baking-dish with the berries; add sugar and pinch of salt, dredge with the flour, and dot with butter. Cover with a somewhat thicker crust than for a pie and bake in a hot oven. Serve cool but not chilled.

FIGS

COMPOTE
(*with port wine*)

1 can preserved figs	2 bitter almonds
1 Tbs. lemon juice	¼ cup port (or red) wine
2 or 3 pieces rind	

Drain syrup from can of figs, put in saucepan with the lemon juice and rind and the almonds, and simmer for a half hour or until reduced by one third. Add figs and wine and bring to a boil. Take out almonds and chill before serving.

COMPOTE WITH SHREDDED ORANGE PEEL

Soak dried white figs overnight. Stew slowly in the same water with 1 tsp. lemon juice, 1 Tbs. orange juice, and 1 Tbs. shredded orange peel, until tender. Arrange them in a shallow pyrex dish, pour over the juice, add a little brown sugar, and place under broiler 3 minutes. Add a little sherry or brandy, if liked, before serving hot or cold.

Fresh Ripe Figs

May be peeled, 1 tsp. honey and a few drops liqueur put on each one, and chilled before serving.

FRUIT JELLIES

Use any recipe for orange, lemon, or tangerine jelly, adding a mixture of cut-up canned or fresh fruit before pouring into mold. Serve with sweetened whipped cream flavored with sherry.

(See recipe for apricot wine jelly, page 188.)

FRUIT SAGO OR TAPIOCA

BASIC RECIPE

3 cups fruit juice to ½ cup
sago or Minute tapioca
1 cup sugar (or less, according to sweetness of fruit)
¼ tsp. salt

Cook sago or tapioca in double boiler with the fruit juice
for a half hour, then add sugar and salt and cook a half hour
longer or until perfectly clear. Turn out in glass bowl and
serve very cold with plain cream, or whipped cream sweetened and flavored, or sweetened with honey.

Good Combinations

Currant juice: see Rote Grütze, page 192.

Pineapple, orange, tangerine, or *grapefruit* juice, and *lemon*
or *lime:* see Goula Malacca, page 205.

Raspberry and *currant:* one half raspberry juice and one
half currant juice.

Rhubarb and *lemon:* add stewed rhubarb and juice and
¼ cup lemon juice (3 cups in all) to tapioca.

Strawberry juice and a few whole strawberries.

CRUSHED FRUIT TAPIOCA

½ cup Minute tapioca
¼ cup water
¾ cup sugar
1 tsp. butter
¼ tsp. salt

1 Tbs. lemon juice
3½ cups crushed fruit and
juice (strawberries, raspberries, blackberries, etc.)

Crush the fruit and let stand with the sugar long enough
to draw the juice. Put the tapioca, water, salt, butter, and
juice drained from the fruit into a double boiler, stir well,
and cook until clear. Add fruit, pour into a glass serving-
dish, and chill.

FRUITS, FRESH OR COOKED

To serve with rice, custards, cheese, etc.:
Red raspberries
Strawberries
Preserved quince
Cut-up peaches
Brandied peaches (with ice cream)
Sherried apricots, peaches, etc.

LEMON

JELLY

(See Fruit Jellies, page 195)

RING MOLD OF LEMON ICE

Pack a ring mold with lemon ice. Turn out and fill center with a mixture of fresh fruit — pineapple, grapefruit, honeydew melon, white grapes, etc., soaked in kirsch.

WATER ICE

(See Water Ices, page 216)

LIME

JELLY

1½ cups lime juice	3 Tbs. gelatine, dissolved in
1 cup sugar	3 Tbs. cold water
3 large leaves of pepper- mint geranium	2 cups water
½ tsp. spinach juice	1 cup fruit (pineapple, grape- fruit, grapes, or melon)
Mint leaves	Rind of 1 lime, grated

Boil sugar and water together for 5 minutes, and pour hot over gelatine and the geranium leaves; cool 5 minutes, strain. Add lime juice with rind of lime and spinach juice. When nearly set, add fruit. Turn into molds and chill. Garnish with whipped cream, geranium, and mint leaves.

WATER ICE

(See Water Ices, page 216)

MELONS

CANTALOUPE, CASABA, HONEYDEW, WATERMELON

(See Fresh Fruits, page 182)

MIXED FRUIT

FRUIT COUPES

Half-fill glasses with any combinations of mixed cut-up fruit, sweetened and flavored with rum or kirsch if liked. Top with a generous tablespoon of lemon, orange, or pineapple ice.

'MÉLI-MÉLO'

Combine pieces of canned apricots with tangerine or orange pulp, a few white grapes, and a little lime or lemon juice. Pour over sherry or kirsch, put in serving glasses and chill. A sprig of mint may be added to each glass.

See also cut-up fresh fruits (page 182).

MINT

JELLY

(with mixed fruit. See Lime Jelly, page 197)

ICE

(with fresh fruit. See Water Ices, page 217)

ORANGES

Cut up and mixed with other fruits. Sherry may be added.

JELLY

(See Fruit Jellies, page 195)

WATER ICE

(See Water Ices, page 217)

PEACHES

BAKED
(with brown sugar)

Scald fresh peaches and remove skins. Cut in half and arrange in pyrex pie dish with a small dab of butter, 1 tsp. brown sugar, and a little nutmeg on each half. Bake in hot oven.

With Orange Rind

Scald fresh peaches and remove skins. Cut in half and arrange in pyrex pie dish. Grate orange rind over the peaches, sprinkle with sugar, and bake in oven. Add about 1 Tbs. curaçao and serve cold.

Canned peaches may be used for the above recipes, in which case use some of the syrup instead of sugar and put under broiler instead of in oven.

COMPOTE

6 ripe peaches	1 cup red wine
6 Tbs. powdered sugar	1 tsp. grated lemon peel
1 in. stick cinnamon	

Pare and slice peaches; sprinkle with powdered sugar and

set aside. Put wine, cinnamon, and lemon peel in a pan, boil 4 or 5 minutes, and strain over peaches. Cover and let stand 2 hours before serving.

WITH KIRSCH

10 ripe peaches   2 cups water
1 cup sugar   ½ cup kirsch

Peel, cut in halves, and stone fruit. Boil water and sugar 10 minutes, removing any scum that rises. Put in fruit carefully and let it simmer, being sure that it does not burn. When liquid is all absorbed, remove from fire; add kirsch and chill.

PEACH CUP

Place brandied peaches in sherbet glasses and cover with vanilla or peach ice cream, frozen not too hard.

PEACHES
(cut up with red raspberries)

PEACH FLAMBÉE

8 peaches
3 cups sugar syrup
½ cup brandy

Dip peaches in boiling water to remove skins. Place in colander over boiling water and steam until thoroughly warm. Place in chafing-dish and pour over them the heated syrup. Add brandy; set it on fire and extinguish just before serving. Almonds, shaved, split and toasted, may be sprinkled over the peaches.

PEACHES ROYAL

2 cups sugar	1 cup wild strawberries
1 cup water	2 Tbs. powdered sugar
6 ripe peaches	2 Tbs. brandy
1 cup heavy cream	

Boil sugar and water 5 minutes. Pare, cut in halves, and cook peaches a few minutes in syrup. Remove, arrange in a glass dish, and chill in refrigerator. Have cream and berries chilled. When ready to serve, mash berries fine, whip cream to a stiff froth while gradually adding powdered sugar and brandy, combining lightly with berries, and put in spoonfuls over peaches.

PEACH PUDDING

Butter a pudding dish and cover the bottom with neat buttered slices of stale bread, from which the crusts have been removed. On each piece place a half ripe peach, skin down. Fill each with 1 tsp. sugar and a small piece of butter and a little nutmeg, occasionally adding more sugar. Bake in moderate oven. Just before serving add 2 Tbs. sherry or any kind of wine. Serve in the same dish, either hot or cold, with cream.

PEACHES IN RED WINE

12 peaches	1 small glass red raspberry
3 cups red wine	and currant jelly
1 cup sugar	

Peel peaches by plunging them first into boiling water, then into cold. Arrange them in a shallow enamel pan side by side and pour over them a syrup made by boiling the wine and sugar together for 5 minutes. Place the pan on the flame and poach the peaches gently until they may be easily pierced with a fork. Let them cook in the syrup, then arrange them on a platter. Now reduce the syrup by boiling rapidly until only 1 cup is left. Remove from fire and add jelly. Stir until melted, then allow it to become quite cold before pouring over the peaches. Serve well chilled.

PEACHES IN WHITE WINE

6 peaches	½ cup sugar
½ cup Sauterne	2 Tbs. butter

Cut peaches in half without peeling. Pour over them the wine and leave to soak for at least an hour. Crack pits and extract kernels. Melt the butter in an enamel saucepan, and when it bubbles put in peaches and sauté lightly. Drain carefully and arrange in serving-dish. Cook the sugar and kernels with the wine in which peaches were soaked, pour over peaches, and serve hot or cold.

PEACH FRAPPÉ

(*See Frozen Desserts, page* 215)

PEACH ICE CREAM

(*See Frozen Desserts, page* 214)

PEACH SHORTCAKE

(*See Shortcakes, page* 213)

PEARS

BAKED NO. I

Pare, core, and bake hard pears in casserole with about 1 in. of sugar water (half and half) and lemon peel. Remove pears and add ½ cup Cointreau or any other liqueur to syrup. Boil 3 minutes and pour over pears, which have been returned to casserole. Serve very cold.

BAKED NO. 2

Cut pears in half without peeling but take out cores. Cook in syrup with lemon peel and a few cloves or a piece of stick cinnamon until half done; then arrange in shallow baking-dish with syrup and put under broiler. Serve in same dish.

COMPOTE
(*with ginger*)

Make a syrup of 2 cups water, 2 cups sugar, and a piece of lemon peel. Cook halves or quarters of firm pears in this until clear, add a little cut-up preserved ginger and ¼ cup ginger syrup, or cook 2 or 3 pieces of crushed green ginger root in the syrup before adding pears.

With Maraschino

Take a can of preserved pears, drain syrup into saucepan, and arrange pears in a glass dish. Add to syrup 2 Tbs. sugar, 1 Tbs. maraschino, and a vanilla bean. Let reduce on fire to one-half quantity; strain over pears and serve cold.

With Red Wine Jelly

First make a syrup by boiling 2 cups of good claret with 1 cup sugar for 5 minutes; then add 6 pears, peeled and left whole. Cook until tender but do not let them lose their shape. Cool, then place in refrigerator to chill.

Now make a wine jelly as follows:

½ cup strained lemon juice	1 cup sugar and
2 Tbs. gelatine, dissolved in	½ cup water
¼ cup cold water	1 cup red wine

Boil sugar and water 1 minute, then add lemon juice,

wine, and gelatine. Pour into a circular ring mold which has been dipped in cold water. When cool place in refrigerator to stiffen. Turn out carefully onto a glass dish and pile the pears in the center. Add ¼ cup port to the wine syrup in which pears were cooked, and pour over all. Serve very cold.

With Wine

8 pears	Juice of 1 lemon
2 cups sugar	2 or 3 pieces of rind
1 cup water	6 cloves
1 cup white wine	

Peel firm pears, leaving stems, and drop into cold water. Place sugar and water in a heavy kettle over slow fire and stir until sugar melts, then drain pears and drop into it. Add lemon juice, rind, and cloves; cover and cook gently till pears are done. Take out with skimmer and place upright in compote dish. Add wine to syrup and cook until it thickens, then pour over pears.

COMPOTE OF DRIED PEARS
(with red wine)

Soak pears in cold water for several hours. Put them in a saucepan with a piece of stick cinnamon; cover them with water and simmer gently covered until they are soft. Pour off the liquid into another saucepan, add a little lemon peel and sugar to taste and several spoonfuls of red wine. Cook 2 or 3 minutes and pour over the pears. Serve cold.

PERSIMMONS

With Orange Juice and Liqueur

Cut very ripe persimmons in quarters part way down. Arrange in fruit dish; pour over 2 Tbs. orange (or tangerine)

juice to each fruit, a squeeze of lemon or lime, and about
1 tsp. of any liqueur. Curaçao and Cointreau are both
good.

PERSIMMON FRAPPÉ

(See Frozen Desserts, page 215)

PERSIMMON ICE CREAM

(See Frozen Desserts, page 214)

PINEAPPLE

With Liqueur

Cut top off of pineapple, cut out pulp, and core. Shred
pulp and marinate with sugar, mint, and liqueur (maraschino or kirsch). Put back in shell and replace top, or fill
shell with pineapple sherbet.

Cut up with other fruit.

PINEAPPLE SHERBET

(See Frozen Desserts, page 216)

PINEAPPLE TAPIOCA (GOULA MALACCA, A PINEAPPLE DESSERT, AS SERVED IN INDIA)

3 cups fruit juice (grapefruit, orange, tangerine, some lime or lemon)	1 cup cane sugar
	½ cup Minute tapioca
	1 shredded ripe pineapple
	¼ tsp. salt
Rind of 2 oranges	Bennett's orange coloring matter

Grate the rind of the oranges into the fruit juice and heat
in a double boiler; add the sugar, salt, and tapioca, stir well,
and cook until clear (about 1 hour). Then add the pulp and

juice of the pineapple and turn into a serving-dish. Place in icebox for several hours and serve with the following sauce. (Anne Stow Fithian.)

Sauce

1 cup honey   1 cup cream

Whip the cream and add honey slowly and continue whipping until thoroughly mixed, as it should be very stiff when served. Put it in a glass pitcher in which it is to be served and place in icebox to chill thoroughly for several hours. This is passed with the dessert and served with a spoon. (Anne Stow Fithian.)

WATER ICE

(See Water Ices, page 217)

PLUMS AND PRUNES

COMPOTE OF PLUMS, PRUNES, AND PEARS WITH RICE MOLD

1 can greengage plums   Ring mold of rice,
1 can pears   cooked with milk
Stewed prunes

Drain syrup from the can of greengage plums, combine with the syrup from the pears and the juice of the prunes. Cook down to one half, adding sugar to taste. Arrange the fruit in and around a ring of rice. Pour over some of the syrup and pass the rest in a sauce boat.

PRUNES BORDEAUX

1 cup stewed prunes   2-in. stick cinnamon
½ cup juice   3 cloves
Grated rind 1 lemon   1 cup Bordeaux wine

Add sugar, lemon rind, cinnamon, and butter to stewed

prunes, and simmer over a very slow fire for 1 hour, shaking the pan occasionally to prevent sticking. When all the liquid is absorbed, add wine. Heat, but do not boil. Serve hot with duck, game, or chicken.

JELLIED PRUNE COMPOTE

1 cup stewed prunes, pitted	1-in. stick cinnamon
1/4 cup juice, sweetened	1 cup boiling water
1/8 tsp. salt	4 Tbs. potato flour
A few cracked pits	1 Tbs. lemon juice

Put in a saucepan the prunes, juice, and crushed pits. Add sugar, salt, cinnamon, and boiling water and simmer 10 minutes. Dilute potato flour with enough cold water to pour easily; add to prune mixture and stir constantly while cooking 5 minutes. Remove cinnamon, add lemon juice, and pour into serving-dish. Chill and serve with cream.

SPICED COMPOTE OF PRUNES AND RAISINS

1 lb. prunes	6 cloves
1/2 lb. seeded raisins (muscatel)	Rind of half a lemon, cut very thin
1 piece stick cinnamon	1/2 cup claret (or 1/4 cup port)

Soak the prunes overnight; simmer in water in which they were soaked until soft. Add raisins, spices, and lemon rind and stew slowly for about an hour. Add the claret or port and serve with meat or as a dessert.

QUINCES

BAKED

Peel and core 5 or 6 quinces to fill a shallow baking-dish; fill holes with sugar. Cook peelings and cores in 2 cups water, reduce to 1 cup; add 1 cup sugar, stir until dissolved. Pour over quinces, cover, and bake in slow oven several hours or until soft.

COMPOTE
(*with apples*)

Use one part apples to three parts quinces. Weigh before cooking. Allow ¾ lb. sugar to 1 lb. fruit. Peel, core, and cut into quarters the quinces and apples and boil in clear water until tender. Take out the fruit with the skimmer and put in the sugar. Boil 5 minutes and skim; then put in the fruit and cook until a dark amber color, about an hour or until tender. 2 Tbs. rum may be added.

ICED COMPOTE
(*with rice*)

3 cups milk	1 Tbs. gelatine, dissolved in a
A little grated lemon rind	little hot water
½ cup rice	1 cup whipped cream, sweetened
1 egg white	A few drops lemon juice
1 saltspoon salt	½ cup sugar

Put milk and the grated lemon rind in a double boiler. When this boils add rice and salt and cook until the rice is tender and the milk nearly boiled away. Stir in stiffly beaten egg white, sugar, and gelatine. Allow the mixture to cool, but before it stiffens fold in the whipped cream and lemon juice. Pour immediately into a ring mold and place in the refrigerator to become firm.

Serve unmolded with the center filled with preserved quinces that have been drained and sliced.

RAISINS

COMPOTE

Soak ½ cup seeded raisins overnight in 1 cup grape juice. Bring slowly to the boil, add a stick of cinnamon and a little sugar to taste, and simmer until the mixture is quite thick. Add a little sherry or red wine. May be served hot or cold with rice, farina, or custard.

SHERRIED

Cook muscatel raisins in sherry in double boiler until they have absorbed all the liquid.

SPICED

(See Prunes, page 207)

WITH APPLES

(See Apples, page 183)

RASPBERRIES (BLACK)

COMPOTE

Cut rather thick slices of stale white bread into ¾-in. pieces. Let dry a while before using. Stew 1 qt. blackcaps with ¾ cup sugar. When the juice begins to run, add the bread and stew until soft. Turn into compote dish and serve very cold with cream or cottage cheese.

BERRY MOLD

Cut slices of bread ½ in. thick; remove the crusts. Fit the slices closely together on the bottom and sides of a plain mold, leaving no spaces. Heat 1 qt. fresh berries with 1 cup sugar until the juice runs freely. Stir until the sugar is dissolved, but do not cook it. Fill the mold to the top, cover with bread slices, and pack in bowl or pan of ice for several hours. Turn out on platter and serve with cream.

Red raspberries or strawberries may be used in place of the blackcaps.

DEEP-DISH TART

(See page 213)

SHORTCAKE

(See page 213)

RASPBERRIES (RED)

COMPOTE
(with wine)

Place **1** qt. raspberries in a bowl, sprinkle with **2** Tbs. sugar and 1 Tbs. kirsch, and mix well. Heat ¾ cup claret with 2 Tbs. powdered sugar and half a stick of cinnamon. Reduce to half the quantity, let cool; strain through cheese-cloth over raspberries. Mix well and serve in a glass dish.

With Peaches

Mix red raspberries with twice the amount of cut-up peaches. Sprinkle with sugar and let stand 20 minutes. A little kirsch or white wine may be added.

ROMANOFF

1 pt. raspberries	⅓ cup powdered sugar
1½ cups heavy cream	¼ cup Kirsch

Use only red ripe raspberries of fine quality. Beat cream to stiff froth, gradually adding sugar and kirsch. Mix lightly with berries; chill and serve in tall thin glasses.

SHORTCAKE

(See page 213)

WATER ICE

(See Water Ices, page 217)

RHUBARB

Directions for Cooking

If possible, use the delicate hothouse rhubarb or thin pink stalks which have been grown in a barrel or forced, so that they are tender and less acid than the usual variety. Cut in 1-in. lengths without peeling. Cook quickly in plenty of water with 1 or 2 thin slices of lemon. Take off stove and add sugar to taste, stirring till all is dissolved. Chill thoroughly. A few pieces of fresh angelica may be cooked with the rhubarb, which gives a delicate flavor, or a few leaves of fresh mint may be used instead.

RHUBARB TAPIOCA

½ cup Minute tapioca (or sago)	2 tsp. lemon juice
	A little lemon peel
3 cups water	1½ cups rhubarb, cut in
⅓ tsp. salt	½-in. pieces
2 Tbs. angelica, cut up	

Cook tapioca in water with salt until clear in double boiler. Add lemon juice, peel, angelica, and rhubarb. Cook until rhubarb is soft; turn out in glass dish and chill. Serve with cream.

STRAWBERRIES

BORDEAUX

Select fine berries, wash and hull. Pour over ¼ cup of claret and sprinkle with sugar to taste. Allow to stand a half hour and serve cold.

CANNELON GLACÉ

2 cups sugar	2 cups fresh strawberry pulp
4 cups water	Juice of 2 lemons
2 Tbs. gelatine	Whipped cream

Make a syrup of the sugar and water. Add gelatine and set aside to cool. When cold, add strawberries and lemon juice. Line a ring mold with the mixture, fill the center with whipped cream, sweetened, to which a little dissolved gelatine has been added, and pack in salt and ice for at least an hour. Serve garnished with sliced strawberries.

COMPOTE

Make a syrup of 1 cup sugar and 1 cup water; add 1 Tbs. potato flour dissolved in a little cold water; stir until the syrup thickens. Pour over sliced berries; chill and serve with cream.

STRAWBERRIES

(served with cheese or rice)

STRAWBERRY ICE CREAM

(See Frozen Desserts, page 214)

SHORTCAKE

Cut up berries (do not mash) and let stand with sugar about a half hour. Allow 2 qts. berries for a full-sized shortcake (biscuit dough) baked in a layer tin. Split and butter while hot; put the berries between and on top, pouring the juice over and around, and serve at once with cream passed separately.

WATER ICE

(See Water Ices, page 217)

DEEP–DISH TARTS

Make a simple piecrust or very rich biscuit dough. Fill pyrex baking-dish with the fruit, add sugar to taste, a pinch of salt, and dredge lightly with flour. Cover with a somewhat thicker crust than for a pie and bake in hot oven. Serve cool but not too cold.

Apple	Blueberries
Apricot	Plums
Blackberries	Sour cherries
Black raspberries	

FRUIT SHORTCAKES

Make a rich biscuit dough without sweetening; bake in layer-cake tins or in individual portions. Split and butter while hot. Put between layers and on top crushed and sweetened berries (2 quart baskets will allow enough fruit so that there will be plenty of juice). Save out some whole berries to garnish the top. Pass cream separately.

Blackberries	Strawberries
Blueberries	Peaches
Black or red raspberries	

FROZEN DESSERTS

ICE CREAMS

General Rules for Freezing

Set temperature regulator at the coldest point. The regulator should be turned back to normal position after 2 or 3 hours, or when ice cream is ready. For the best freezing results, each tray should be in direct contact with the super-freezer; this is accomplished by putting 2 or 3 tablespoons of water on floor of the super-freezer, then placing tray in, or by having the bottom of the tray wet.

When mixture starts to freeze, beat with egg beater every 20 minutes until too thick for beater; then spoon the ice cream carefully from edges to middle as it freezes quickly around sides. When it reaches this stage, be careful not to disturb too much.

PEACH ICE CREAM

2 cups peach pulp, mashed	½ cup sugar and
2 cups cream	¾ cup water, boiled to a syrup
1 egg yolk	which will string

Heat cream in double boiler and pour over beaten egg yolk; then return to double boiler and cook, stirring until smooth. Cool and add syrup, which has been cooled, and ½ tsp. salt, and put in refrigerator tray. Add peaches just before beating for last time.

PERSIMMON ICE CREAM

6 or 7 very ripe persimmons	½ cup sugar and
2 cups cream	¾ cup water, boiled to a syrup
1 egg yolk	which will string
½ tsp. salt	Juice 1 lemon (or 2 limes)

Peel and remove stem and core of persimmons and press through coarse sieve with lemon (or lime) juice and salt.

Heat cream in double boiler and pour over beaten egg yolk, then return to double boiler and cook, stirring until smooth. Cool and add syrup, which has been cooled and put in refrigerator tray. Add persimmons just before beating for last time.

STRAWBERRY ICE CREAM

2 qt. boxes strawberries	½ cup sugar and
2 cups cream	¾ cup water, boiled to a syrup
½ tsp. salt	which will string
1 egg yolk	

Prepare strawberries, sprinkle with sugar, and let stand

for a few minutes; then crush through a strainer and add salt.

Heat cream in double boiler and pour over beaten egg yolk, then return to double boiler and cook, stirring until smooth. Cool and add syrup which has been cooled, and put in refrigerator tray. Add strawberries just before beating for last time.

MOUSSE

PEACH MOUSSE

1 package frozen peaches	1½ cups heavy cream
¾ cup sugar	1 tsp. vanilla

Crush peaches with a silver fork; add sugar and chill. Whip cream and add vanilla. Fold in and turn into tray of automatic refrigerator with control set at coldest point and freeze 2 or 3 hours, or until as firm as desired.

This is greatly improved by adding a teaspoonful of kirsch to each serving.

Strawberries or red raspberries may be used instead.

FRAPPÉS

PEACH FRAPPÉ

Take 12 ripe peaches (for 4 people), peel, and mash through colander. Sweeten to taste; add ½ cup sherry and pack in ice for 1½ to 2 hours (not in a refrigerator tray). It should not be frozen stiff and should be stirred once or twice. Serve in glasses.

PERSIMMON FRAPPÉ

Take 6 or 7 very ripe persimmons, peel, and mash through colander. Add ⅛ tsp. salt, sweeten to taste, flavor with 1 Tbs. curaçao, 2 Tbs. orange juice, and 1 tsp. lemon (or lime) juice. Pack in ice for 1½ to 2 hours (not in a refrigerator tray). It should not be frozen stiff and should be stirred once or twice. Serve in glasses.

SHERBETS

ITALIAN SHERBET

Make a syrup of 2 cups sugar and 1 cup water. Cool, add ½ cup lemon juice, 1 cup orange juice, and 4 cups peach or any fruit pulp; pass through sieve. Sherry or any liqueur may be added. Pour into mold and pack in ice and salt for about 3 hours, or put in refrigerator tray.

PINEAPPLE SHERBET

Use a large pineapple with good foliage. Cut off top to form a lid and scoop out the inside of the fruit. Shred the pineapple pulp and add to it, 1 cup orange juice, ½ cup lemon juice, and sugar to taste. Let stand for a half hour, then press through a coarse sieve. Freeze until firm, then fill scooped out pineapple with the sherbet, piling it high and perching the foliage on top. Kirsch or maraschino may be added.

WATER ICES

BASIC RECIPE

1 cup water to 1 cup sugar (or ½ cup sugar if no lemon juice is used). Boil together 5 minutes. Cool and combine with 3 cups fruit juice. This is better frozen in an old-fashioned ice-cream freezer.

LEMON OR LIME

2 cups juice, a little grated rind. Combine with syrup (2 cups sugar and 2 cups water boiled together).

MINT

Make a lemon ice, boiling a large bunch of mint leaves with the syrup. Strain; add to juice with a few drops green coloring. Serve with mint leaves.

ORANGE

Two and one-half cups juice, ½ cup lemon, grated rind. Combine with syrup (1 cup sugar and 1 cup water boiled together).

PINEAPPLE

Shred pineapple to make 3 cups after straining. Add 1 Tbs. lemon juice. Combine with syrup (1 cup sugar and 1 cup water boiled together).

RED RASPBERRY

Mash berries through strainer to make 3 cups. Combine with syrup (¾ cup sugar and 1 cup water).

STRAWBERRY

Mash berries through strainer to make 3 cups. Combine with syrup (1 cup sugar and 1 cup water).

TANGERINE

3 cups pure juice, a little grated rind. Combine with syrup.

CHAPTER XIII

MISCELLANEOUS

Candies, Conserves, Herb Vinegars, Honey and Its Uses, Seed Breads, Seed Cakes and Cookies

MENUS

LIST OF RECIPES

CANDIES
  Candied Angelica Stems
  Candied Borage Stars
  Candied Lovage Root
  Sweet Flagroot
  Candied Mint Leaves
  Horehound Candy
    No. 1
    No. 2

HERB JAMS AND JELLIES
  Apple Butter
  Apple Chutney (Cashmere)
  Herb Jellies (Basic Recipe)
    Sweet Geranium
    Sage
    Rosemary
    Tarragon
  Apple Mint Jelly
  Spiced Apple Jelly
  Barberry Jelly
  Elderberry Jam
  Elderberry Jelly
  Green Grape and Mint Jelly
  Gooseberry Chutney
  Rhubarb and Angelica Jam

HERB VINEGARS
  General Directions
  Elder Flower
  Garlic
  Mint
  Mixed Herbs

HONEY AND ITS USES
  Varieties of Honey
  Recipes
    Baked Squash
    Baked or Scalloped Sweet Po
      tatoes
    Bran and Honey Muffins
    Butter Honey Cake
    Hard Honey Cake (Honig
      kuchen)
    Honey Oatmeal Wafers
  Desserts
    Honeyed Apples
    Bar le Duc Currants
    Baked Honey Custard
    Boiled Honey Custard
    Honey Charlotte Russe
    Honey Mousse
    Honey Sauce

CANDIES

CANDIED ANGELICA STEMS

Cut into pieces 4 in. long. Steep for 12 hours in salt and water. Put a layer of cabbage leaves in a clean saucepan, then a layer of angelica, then another layer of leaves on the top. Cover with 4 parts water to 1 part cider vinegar. Boil slowly till the angelica becomes quite green, then strain and weigh the stems.

Allow 1 lb. loaf sugar to each pound of stems. Put the sugar in a clean pan with water to cover; boil 10 minutes and pour this syrup over the angelica. Stand for 12 hours. Pour off the syrup, boil it up for 5 minutes, and pour it again over the angelica. Repeat this process, and after the angelica has stood in the syrup 12 hours, put all on the fire in the saucepan and boil until tender. Take out the pieces of angelica, put them in a jar and pour the syrup over them, or dry them on a sieve and sprinkle them with sugar. They then form candy.

CANDIED BORAGE STARS

Pick the five-petaled blue corollas before they fall. Clean and dry them in a towel. Brush with white of egg, using a small camel's-hair brush, and dredge with fine granulated sugar, using a shaker. Lay on waxed paper and dry in cool place.

CANDIED LOVAGE ROOT

Dig root in the fall, when it is fully ripe. Clean, scrape, and cut crosswise into sections. Boil gently in water to cover for several hours, changing several times. Pour off the water and crystallize the root sections in a boiling sugar syrup made by adding 2 cups granulated sugar to ½ cup water. Boil to 300° F. When sections of the root are clear, lift them carefully and spread on buttered paper. Granulated sugar may be sifted over the pieces. (This is an old rule of the Shakers.) Leave in the oven until thoroughly dry and pack in boxes. (Helen N. Webster.)

SWEET FLAGROOT

Prepare the same as lovage, above.

CANDIED MINT LEAVES

Take spearmint or peppermint leaves, picking out the largest and most perfect. Clean and dry them on a towel. Brush with white of egg, using a small camel's-hair brush, and dredge with fine granulated sugar, using a shaker. Lay on waxed paper and dry in a cool place.

HOREHOUND CANDY NO. I

Put one handful of freshly cut horehound leaves into a saucepan with 1½ cups of water, let boil 15 minutes; strain and add 2 lbs. brown sugar. When sugar is dissolved, let it cook gently, without stirring, until a little dropped into cold water will form a hard, rubbery ball. Remove, pour into buttered tins, and cut into squares when nearly cold.

HOREHOUND CANDY NO. 2

Steep 1 oz. of dried horehound herb — leaf, stem and flowers — 2 minutes in 2½ qts. water. Strain and squeeze through cheesecloth and allow the tea to settle. Then decant. Add 3 cups granulated sugar, 1 tsp. cream of tartar to 2 cups of horehound tea.

Boil to 240° F., add 1 tsp. butter, and continue boiling without stirring until the temperature reaches 312°. Remove from fire and add 1 tsp. lemon juice. Pour into a buttered pan. When cool, block in squares, roll in confectionery sugar, and pack in airtight jars. (Helen N. Webster.)

CONSERVES

HERB JAMS AND JELLIES

APPLE BUTTER

3 gals. cider, boiled
down to 1½ gals.
Brown sugar to taste
(about 3 lbs.)

1 bu. tart apples) washed and cut
½ bu. sweet apples) up in pieces
Cinnamon

Unless you have a very large kettle, divide the boiled cider between two smaller ones. Put the apples, a few at a time, part sweet and part sour, in each kettle. Cook slowly, stirring frequently with a wooden spoon until soft and mushy. This will take hours. When the apples cook down and become dark in color, dip out with a 2-qt. saucepan or large dipper, and press with a wooden potato masher through a coarse strainer or colander into smaller kettles. Sweeten to taste and add as much cinnamon as liked, stirring well. Cook down to a thick mush and store in crocks or jars.

APPLE CHUTNEY (CASHMERE)

1 lb. brown sugar	1 pt. cider vinegar
1 lb. Sultana raisins	1 onion, chopped
1 lb. dates	1 Tbs. minced garlic
¼ lb. preserved ginger	1 Tbs. salt
2 lbs. green apples, peeled and cut up	½ tsp. cayenne pepper (or 2 chili peppers)

Stone and cut dates. Boil onion, garlic, and apples in vinegar until tender; then add all the other ingredients and boil together 10 minutes. Seal in jars.

HERB JELLIES: BASIC RECIPE

Prepare apple juice for the jellies by washing the apples, cutting them up and cooking with water until soft. Turn into jelly bag and let drip overnight without squeezing. Crabapples may be used, as well as any tart apple. Measure the juice and for each cup allow 1 Tbs. boiled cider vinegar, ¾ cup sugar, 2 drops essential oil of herb flavor desired, or 1 sprig of the fresh herb. Boil the apple juice 15 minutes with the fresh herbs and the vinegar. Heat the sugar and add to the juice, stirring well until dissolved. Boil about 5 minutes or until it jells easily. If the essential oil is used, add it after the kettle is removed from the stove; stir well and pour into hot glasses.

Sweet geranium	Sage
Rosemary	Tarragon

When flavoring with sweet geranium, a small leaf may be put in the bottom of the jelly glass, 1 tsp. of the hot jelly poured on and allowed to set; then fill the glass.

For Lemon Geranium, use a little lemon juice instead of vinegar.

APPLE MINT JELLY

4 cups strained apple juice
3 cups sugar
Large bunch of mint

Place the sugar on shallow plates in the oven to heat.

Set the fruit juice over the fire with the crushed leaves and stems from mint; let cook for 20 minutes and strain into a clean saucepan. Heat to the boiling point, add the hot sugar, and let cook until the syrup jells. Tint very delicately with spinach juice or green-colored paste and store in jelly glasses. Serve with roast duck or lamb.

SPICED APPLE JELLY

1 cup mild cider vinegar	¾ cup sugar to each cup liquid
4 cups apple juice	Small bag of spices (cloves, mace, and stick cinnamon)

Make jelly as usual, cooking the juice with the vinegar and the spice bag, and straining again before pouring into glasses.

BARBERRY JELLY

Gather berries before they are overripe on a dry day. Wash, strip from stalks, and put on fire in kettle. Crush to start juice, cook till juice runs freely, and then let drip overnight in jelly bag.

Prepare apple juice by cooking cut-up sour apples with cold water to cover until apples are soft enough to mash. Let drip in jelly bag overnight and combine with barberry juice, allowing 1 cup barberry to ½ cup apple. Boil 15 minutes. Allow ¾ cup sugar to each cup fruit juice; heat in oven, add to kettle, stir till dissolved. Boil 5 minutes; test by putting a little on saucer in icebox. When it jells, pour into glasses.

ELDERBERRY JAM

Pick elderberries not too ripe on a dry day. Wash, strip from stems, and weigh. Allow ½ lb. apples cut up into small pieces to every pound of berries. Cook the berries and apples together, adding 1 tsp. salt and a little cold water if necessary, crushing and stirring frequently until soft enough to mash through coarse strainer or colander. Measure and allow ¾ lb. sugar to each cup pulp. Cook all together, stirring constantly, about 20 minutes or until right consistency to stiffen.

ELDERBERRY JELLY

Gather berries before they are overripe on a dry day. Wash, strip from stalks, and put on fire in kettle. Crush to start juice, cook till juice runs freely, then let drip overnight in jelly bag.

Prepare apple juice by cooking cut-up sour apples with cold water to cover until apples are soft enough to mash. Let drip in jelly bag overnight and combine with elderberry juice, allowing 1 cup elderberry to ½ cup apple. Boil 15 minutes. Allow ¾ cup sugar to each cup fruit juice; heat in oven, add to kettle, stir till dissolved. Boil 5 minutes; test by putting a little on saucer in icebox. When it jells, pour into glasses.

GREEN GRAPE AND MINT JELLY

Gather wild grapes before they color; wash and put them in a kettle with just enough water to keep from burning. Cook until the juice runs freely, then allow to drip overnight in jelly bag. Measure the juice and allow ¾ cup sugar to each cup juice. Heat sugar in oven. Put juice in kettle; add a large bunch of fresh mint. Boil 10 minutes, then take out mint; add sugar and stir until dissolved. Boil about 10 minutes or until it jells.

GOOSEBERRY CHUTNEY

3 pts. green gooseberries	½ saltspoon cayenne pepper
¼ lb. dates	½ saltspoon turmeric
¼ lb. raisins	1 clove garlic
1 lb. onions	A little ginger root
¾ lb. brown sugar	1 Tbs. ginger
2 pts. vinegar	1 Tbs. mustard

Cut up ingredients fine and place with spices in preserving kettle. Cover with the vinegar. Simmer 1 to 3 hours or until very soft. Bottle while hot.

RHUBARB AND ANGELICA JAM

Cut rhubarb into inch-length pieces; weigh and allow ¾ lb. sugar to each pound rhubarb. Put in kettle with sugar, a little lemon juice, and a few tender stalks of angelica, cut into small pieces. Cook down to a thick jam, stirring frequently. Put in glasses and seal.

HERB VINEGARS

General Directions

Use fresh herbs. Strip leaves and pack in quart jars about three-fourths full. Heat white wine or cider vinegar to boiling point; fill jars, cover, and let steep for 1 to 2 weeks. Strain into bottles and cork tightly.

Basil
Rosemary } All prepared as above.
Tarragon

For *Red Basil Vinegar*, use red instead of white wine vinegar. This gives it a beautiful color.

ELDER FLOWER VINEGAR

Gather elder flowers on a sunny day; pluck from their stalks and dry quickly and thoroughly on trays above the stove or in oven with open door. Weigh after drying and pack in quart jars, allowing 1 lb. flowers to each pint vinegar. White wine is the best.

Heat vinegar to the boiling point and pour over flowers; cover jars tightly and keep in a warm place for 8 to 9 days, shaking from time to time. Strain through filter paper, bottle, and seal. This is very good with a fruit salad such as pear or apple.

GARLIC VINEGAR

Crush 6 cloves garlic and put them into a glass jar with a little salt. Heat 1 pt. cider or wine vinegar, pour into jar and let stand about 2 weeks. Strain before using.

MINT VINEGAR

1 qt. white-wine vinegar	2 cups spearmint leaves
1 cup sugar	and young tips

Bring the vinegar to a boil; add sugar and mint. Stir, crush, and boil 5 minutes. Strain and bottle while hot. A good flavor for iced tea or fruit punches.

MIXED HERB VINEGAR

1 large handful tarragon	8 shallots, cut up
1 oz. elder flowers	1 clove garlic
(without stems)	4 cloves
½ oz. spearmint or orange	2 peppercorns
mint	2 tps. salt
½ oz. lemon balm	2 qts. white wine vinegar

Heat the vinegar, pour over ingredients, cover and let stand 2 weeks, stirring occasionally. Strain and filter.

HONEY AND ITS USES

Honey has its place in a book on herb cookery, as almost all varieties derive their distinctive flavor from *herbs*, in mixture with blossoms of all kinds, wild and cultivated. Honey has a long and honorable history, and was the sole source of sweetening for the ancients. It was considered of great medicinal value by them, and also played an important rôle in religious rites. The mysterious bee was considered 'sacred' and was celebrated in the writings of Hesiod, Homer, Virgil, and other poets of antiquity. Although sugar was extensively cultivated in the Nile Delta, honey continued to be the only source of sweetening for Europeans until after the discovery of America. Early in the sixteenth century sugar cane was introduced into the West Indies, but honey still played an important part in the diet of the people and bee-keeping was universal. As a natural sweet it is not only wholesome and mildly laxative but contains mineral substances lacking in the white cane sugar of today, from which all the minerals and vitamins have been removed by the process of refining.

Honey, in addition to the vitamins, contains iron, lime, magnesia, and phosphorus in small quantities, and its food value, cup for cup, is about the same as sugar, consisting approximately of 4 parts sugar to 1 part water. The flavor and aroma of honey depend naturally upon the variety of blossoms from which the nectar is obtained. The nectar of each kind of flower contains a distinctive combination of oils and other substances which give the blossoms their special fragrance, and the honey its flavor. As it is almost impossible to prevent bees from visiting more than one kind of flower during a given period, most honeys are made from a mixture of different flavors. However, when the hives are situated near a large supply of one kind of blossom, that distinctive flavor and aroma usually predominates and the product is known by the name of that particular flower (apple, clover, sage, etc.).

In the following list will be found some of the best-known varieties, which, however, vary in flavor and color according to the locality and the season of the year.

ALFALFA

An important source of honey supply in the Midwest.

APPLE BLOSSOM

During a short period many orchardists rent hives for the apple-blossom season in order to assure the pollination of the blossom. The result is a delicate and delicious honey for which, notably, the Shenandoah Valley is famed.

'ATTIC' (HONEY OF HYMETTUS)

In ancient Greece the most famous variety of honey came from Mount Hymettus, where the wild thyme grew in profusion. It is thought that the so-called honey of Hymettus, sold nowadays in attractive little pots, bears little or no relation to that of ancient Greece, but it is nevertheless delicious.

BASSWOOD (AMERICAN LINDEN)

This is the greatest honey-yielding tree in America, and lends its flavor to many varieties.

BUCKWHEAT

Dark and strong in flavor, but excellent in mixture with other late-summer blossoms.

CLOVER (WHITE)

Light in color, mild, and delicate; good for recipes in which no strong or distinctive flavor is desired.

GOLDENROD

Predominates in late-summer honey; usually dark and aromatic.

HEATHER

A variety less known in this country but highly esteemed in Great Britain and Europe.

'MIXED HERBS' AND FLOWERS

If hives are kept near a flower or herb garden, the result is a pleasant mixture with an elusive flavor difficult to analyze.

NARBONNE (WHITE, GRANULAR)

A famous honey in which the flavors of rosemary, wild thyme, and various members of the mint family are mingled.

ORANGE

Product of California and Florida. Distinctive and sometimes too sweetly reminiscent of the heavy scent of orange blossoms.

SAGE

California. Aromatic and distinctive. Sometimes lacking in delicacy.

WILD HONEY

Has usually a strong, rank flavor, highly esteemed in olden times.

HONEY IN COOKING

Honey should never be kept in the icebox but in a dry, warm place. A shelf in the kitchen pantry is ideal. In the case of strained honey, if it is to be kept any length of time, it should be pasteurized to prevent fermentation. We can be fairly certain that there is little or no adulteration in the honey we buy, since government regulations and inspection are very strict. In the case of comb honey, adulteration is altogether too difficult and expensive to be worth while and one may feel quite certain that it is the genuine article.

Honey may be used in place of sugar in almost all recipes for cookies, especially those calling for spices and nuts. Perhaps the most famous honey cakes are those made in Nuremburg at Christmas time, known as Honigkuchen, Lebkuchen, Pfeffernüsse, etc.

In substituting honey for sugar, a safe rule is to use cup for cup or perhaps a little less honey than cane sugar. As honey has a greater liquid content than sugar, that factor should be taken into consideration in adding milk, water, or other liquids.

Honey cakes keep better when butter is not used, but are usually not so good to the taste.

The following recipes have been tried and found good.

RECIPES

BAKED SQUASH

Cut Hubbard or other hard-shelled squash into individual portions, put 1 tsp. butter and 1 Tbs. honey on each one and bake in oven.

BAKED OR SCALLOPED SWEET POTATOES

Honey may be used in place of sugar in scalloped sweet potatoes, or a little may be spread on slices when grilling or frying.

BRAN AND HONEY MUFFINS

½ cup honey
1 cup flour
¼ to ½ tsp. soda
¼ tsp. salt
2 cups bran

2 Tbs. melted butter
1½ cups milk
¾ cup finely chopped English walnuts,
  or ½ cup chopped raisins

Sift together the flour, soda, and salt and mix them with the bran. Add the other ingredients and bake for 25 or 30 minutes in a hot oven in gem tins. This will make 16 large muffins, each of which may be considered roughly to be a 100-calorie portion and to contain 2 grams of protein.

BUTTER HONEY CAKE

1 cup honey
½ cup butter
½ tsp. ginger
½ tsp. cinnamon
1 tsp. ground cardamom seed
¼ cup sour cream

2½ cups flour
½ to 1 tsp. soda
1 oz. candied orange peel
1 cup seeded raisins
3 eggs

Cream butter and add honey. Add egg yolks unbeaten. Beat mixture thoroughly, and add the flour sifted with spices and soda and sour cream. Add fruit and mix well; then add the whites of eggs which have been beaten until stiff. Bake 30 minutes in moderate oven.

HARD HONEY CAKE ('HONIGKUCHEN')

¾ cup honey
½ cup sugar
3½ to 4 cups flour
1 egg
¼ cup brandy or rum
3 Tbs. chopped candied orange peel
3 Tbs. chopped candied lemon peel
¼ tsp. ginger

½ tsp. powdered cardamom
⅛ tsp. powdered cloves
1 tsp. cinnamon
½ tsp. soda, dissolved in 1
  tsp. warm water
6 Tbs. ground sweet almonds
1 Tbs. ground bitter almonds
Pinch of salt

Put honey and sugar in saucepan and bring slowly to a

boil. Remove and cool slightly, then stir in almonds, orange, and lemon peel, well beaten egg, spices, brandy or rum, and soda. Work in flour to make a firm dough that can be kneaded. Knead well and roll to about ¼-in. thickness. Cut into oblong shapes (about 2 × 4 in.). Brush with egg white and bake in moderate oven. Keep in tin box 3 to 4 weeks before using.

HONEY OATMEAL WAFERS

1 cup rolled oats, or ⅔ cup oats and ⅓ cup chopped nuts	2 tsp. melted butter
⅓ cup honey	⅓ tsp. salt
1 egg	¼ tsp. vanilla

Beat egg until light; add honey, continuing to beat, then remaining ingredients. Drop on a well-greased baking-sheet by teaspoonfuls about 2 in. apart. Flatten slightly with a knife dipped in cold water and bake in moderate oven (350° F.) until a delicate brown (about 10 minutes).

DESSERTS

BAKED APPLES
(sweetened with honey. See Chapter XII)

HONEYED APPLES

2 qts. apples, cut into small pieces	1 cup vinegar
2 cups honey	1 tsp. cinnamon

Heat the honey, vinegar, and cinnamon together and cook the apples, a few at a time, in the syrup until they become transparent. Pour the syrup which remains after all the fruit is cooked over the apples.

BAR LE DUC CURRANTS

Remove seeds from currants by cutting a small slit in the side of each currant and remove the seeds by means of a needle. After this is done, weigh the currants and take an equal weight of honey. Bring the honey to the boiling point, add the currants, and allow them to cook at the boiling point for 2 or 3 minutes, or until the skins are tender, being careful not to let the mixture boil violently, because this is likely to destroy the shape of the fruit. If the currants are so juicy as to liquify the honey too much, they may be removed and the syrup reduced to the desired consistency, after which the currants may be replaced.

It is possible, of course, to preserve the currants in honey according to the same recipe without the removal of the seeds, but the preserve thus obtained is not nearly so delicate as when the seeds are removed.

FIGS

(with honey.   See Chapter XII)

GRAPEFRUIT

(with honey.   See Chapter XII)

HONEY CUSTARDS

Baked

3 eggs	⅛ tsp. powdered cinnamon
⅓ cup honey	⅛ tsp. salt
4 cups scalded milk	Nutmeg

Beat the eggs sufficiently to unite the yolks and whites, but not enough to make them foamy. Add the other ingredients and bake in cups or in a large pan in a moderate oven. The baking-dishes should be set in water. Cool and turn out onto a platter, sprinkle with nutmeg, and serve with thick cream.

Boiled

2 cups milk	⅓ cup honey
3 egg yolks	⅛ tsp. salt

Mix the honey, eggs, and salt. Scald the milk and pour it over the eggs. Cook in a double boiler until the mixture thickens. This custard is suitable for use in place of cream on gelatin desserts, or to be poured over sliced oranges or stewed fruit.

HONEY CHARLOTTE RUSSE

1 qt. cream	½ cup delicately flavored honey
6 ladyfingers	2 Tbs. rum or kirsch

Chill the honey by placing the dish containing it in a pan of ice-water. Whip the cream and add it to the honey, mixing the two well, then add the liqueur. Line a dish with ladyfingers and fill it with the honey, cream, and liqueur. Serve very cold.

HONEY MOUSSE

4 eggs	1 cup hot, delicately
1 pint cream	flavored honey

Beat the eggs slightly and slowly pour over them the hot honey. Cook until the mixture thickens. When it is cool, add the cream whipped. Put the mixture into a mold, pack in salt and ice, and let it stand 3 or 4 hours.

HONEY SAUCE
(*See Goula Malacca, page* 205)

SEED BREADS

SWEDISH BOLLER

1 cake yeast	⅓ cup butter (or lard)
¼ cup sugar	1 cup raisins
2 cups milk	¼ cup citron
8 cups sifted flour	4 cardamom seeds
2 eggs	

Dissolve the yeast and sugar in milk which has been scalded and cooled to *lukewarm*. Add the flour to make a sponge. Beat well. Cover and let rise until double in bulk, about 1½ hours. When well risen, add unbeaten eggs with butter and mix until thoroughly blended. Sift remaining flour onto citron and raisins (these may be omitted). Shell cardamom seeds and crush to a fine flour (¼ tsp. cinnamon may be substituted for cardamom if desired), and add with flour, raisins, and citron to first mixture. Cover and let rise until double in bulk, about 1½ hours. Turn out onto a molding-board and shape into biscuits, place on a greased baking-sheet 1 in. apart, and bake in a moderately hot oven (375° F.) for 20 minutes.

SWEDISH COFFEE BREAD

2 cups milk	1½ tsp. salt
1 cake yeast	20 cardamom seeds, shelled and
1 cup sugar	pounded fine
¼ cup lard, or butter	7½ to 8 cups sifted flour

Scald the milk in the top of a double boiler. Take out ½ cup of the milk, and *when lukewarm* add the yeast to soften. To the hot milk add the sugar, shortening, salt, and cardamom seeds. When cool, add yeast. Stir the liquid ingredients into the flour and mix well. Knead for 10 to 15 minutes until the dough springs back into place when pressed with the fingers. Put the dough into a greased bowl, grease the top, cover, and keep warm until double in bulk. The dough may be divided if desired and one half made into a braided loaf and the other half into fancy shaped rolls.

For the Swedish coffee braid, cut the dough into 3 or 4 long pieces of uniform size and roll between the palms of the hands until smooth and even; then braid. Place in a greased pan, cover, let rise, brush with the yolk of an egg slightly beaten and diluted with ½ Tbs. water. Sprinkle with sugar or ground nuts (if desired) and bake in a moderate oven 350° F. for about 45 minutes.

For the fancy rolls, take small pieces of dough, roll between the hands, shape into knots, half moons, or curls, and finish in the same way as the braid. Bake for 20 to 25 minutes in a moderate oven (350° F.).

GINGERBREAD

½ cup brown sugar	1½ cups flour
1 cup dark molasses	1 tsp. ginger
⅜ cup butter	¼ tsp. cinnamon
1 tsp. soda	2 tsp. coriander seeds (or ¼ tsp.
½ cup sour milk	cardamom seeds), crushed
1 egg	

Cream the butter and sugar, stir in the egg, beaten slightly, then the molasses, the soda dissolved in the sour milk, the spices and coriander (or cardamom) seeds, and the flour. Bake in oven, 350° to 375° F. Turn down toward the last.

SEED CAKES AND COOKIES

OLD-FASHIONED SEED CAKE

2 cups sifted cake flour	½ tsp. salt
1 cup butter	½ tsp. mace or nutmeg
1 cup sugar	2 Tbs. caraway seeds
3 eggs, separated	

Mix and sift flour, salt, and nutmeg together three times.

Cream butter, add sugar and cream well together. Add egg yolks, one at a time, beating until blended after each addition. Stir in stiffly beaten egg whites and then add flour, beating until smooth. Add caraway seeds and beat 3 minutes. Turn into shallow loaf pan (6 × 10 × 1 in.) and bake in moderate oven (350° F.) three-quarters of an hour. Cool and serve cut in very thin slices.

ALMOND COOKIES WITH CARDAMOM SEEDS

½ cup butter
1 egg, well beaten
½ cup almonds, blanched
  and finely chopped
½ cup sugar
2 cups flour

1 tsp. cinnamon
1 tsp. cloves
1 tsp. nutmeg
2 Tbs. cardamom seed
Grated rind ½ lemon
1 Tbs. rum

Cream butter, add egg, almonds, and other ingredients, mixed and sifted with flour. Chill. Roll lightly and quickly on slightly floured board or cloth until ¼ in. thick. Cut out with floured cutter and arrange (with spatula) on buttered cooky sheet and bake in moderate oven (325° F.).

SESAME WAFERS

⅓ cup butter
¾ cup sugar
1¼ cups flour
1 tsp. baking powder

1 egg
1 tsp. vanilla
2 Tbs. milk
Sesame seeds

Cream butter and sugar, then add well-beaten egg and milk; then flour sifted with baking powder, and last the vanilla. Spread on bottom of oblong bread tin, very thin, with a wet knife. Sprinkle with sesame seeds which have been first parched in the oven. Bake in hot oven and cut in inch strips while hot, then turn over on rolling pin to form half circles. Or the mixture may be dropped in spoonfuls on a baking sheet and sprinkled with the sesame seeds.

SEED COOKIES
Aniseed — Caraway — Cardamom — Sesame

The above recipe may be used for rolled out cookies, in which case add enough flour to roll out, chill in refrigerator. Then roll very thin on well-floured board, sprinkle with seeds, and bake in moderate oven. This recipe may be varied according to taste, by substituting 1 Tbs. brandy for one of the milk (especially recommended for aniseed cookies) and adding a little grated lemon or orange peel. Sesame seed should always be parched in the oven, and cardamom slightly crushed.

BLITZ KUCHEN

4 eggs	½ lb. flour
½ lb. butter	Juice and rind of 1 lemon
½ lb. sugar	

For Top

1½ cups almonds, chopped fine   ¾ cup sugar
1 tsp. cinnamon and ¼ tsp. crushed cardamom seed

Cream the butter, add the sugar, beating well, then the eggs, well beaten, flour, lemon juice and grated rind. Spread very thin with a knife or spatula, on a baking sheet, and sprinkle with the almonds, spices, and sugar mixed together.

Bake until golden yellow and cut in diamond shapes while hot.

GINGER WAFERS

1 cup butter	¼ tsp. crushed cardamom seed
½ cup sugar	1 tsp. soda, dissolved in
½ cup dark molasses	½ cup boiling water
1 tsp. cinnamon	2 cups flour
1 tsp. ginger	Pinch salt

Cream the butter, add sugar and molasses, beating well. Add soda, then the flour sifted together with spices and salt. Drop by spoonfuls on a baking sheet and bake in moderate oven.

MENUS

LUNCHEON

1

Egg timbales with tomato sauce (p. 94)
(Cold meat)   Beet and watercress salad (p. 152) — cheese
Mixed fruit   Sesame wafers (p. 237)

2

Tomato cocktail (p. 174)   Savory cheese rolls (p. 164)
Chicken livers with saffron rice (p. 104)   Mixed green salad
Fruit sago (p. 196)

3

Hors d'oeuvre
Omelet with fine herbs (p. 88)
Mixed vegetable salad — cheese
Rhubarb compote (p. 211)   Seed Cake (p. 236)

4

Savory cheese ring (p. 166)
Tomato and avocado salad
Berry Mold (p. 209)

5 [1]

Jellied tomato soup
Cold salmon — mayonnaise   Cold vegetables
Pineapple ice with mint

6

Carrot timbale with green peas (p. 124)
Ripe pear salad — cheese

These luncheon menus can be varied indefinitely and easily
elaborated for 'company' by adding an extra course — hors
d'oeuvre or soup — and by serving cold meat with the salad.

[1] A hot weather menu.

DINNERS

1

Sorrel soup (p. 29)
Roast leg of lamb with rosemary (p. 54)
Boiled new potatoes with fine herbs
Peas 'à la française' (p. 137)
Salad
Strawberry cannelon (p. 212)

2

French herb soup (p. 18)
Braised beef with vegetables (p. 46)   Beet greens
Currant and raspberry sago (p. 196)

3

Essence of celery, hot or cold
Artichokes in casserole (p. 116)
Chicken au vin blanc (p. 70)   Mixed green salad
Creamy rice with fresh raspberries

4

Rosemary soup (p. 29)
Ragout de veau (p. 57)   Saffron rice (p. 104)
Spinach — Purée of carrots with mint (p. 124)
Baked peaches (p. 199)

5

Hors d'oeuvre
Braised duck in casserole (p. 71)   Orange and romaine salad
Raspberry compote (p. 209) — cheese

6

Potage santé (p. 28)
Filet of sole au vin blanc (p. 42)
New potatoes with fine herbs
Savory string beans — Green salad
Deep-dish cherry tart — cheese

These dinner menus can be simplified by leaving out soup, or made more elaborate by adding either a vegetable entrée or a salad. Some of the soup recipes are hearty enough to serve in a tureen — as the main dish — followed by a vegetable salad with cheese, and fruit for dessert.

CHAPTER XIV

LEFT-OVER DISHES

LIST OF RECIPES

SOUP

Combine any odds and ends of vegetables, meat, etc., including at least ½ cup liquid. Reduce to pulp in Waring mixer, put in double boiler with milk, season and bring to a boil.

FISH

SALMON KEDGEREE

Combine flaked cooked salmon with boiled rice, one or two hard-cooked eggs, butter, and cream. Cook in double boiler a few minutes and turn out on platter.

LOBSTER OR CRAB

Flake fine, combine with soufflé, and bake in moderate oven.

ANY KIND OF LEFT-OVER FISH

Mix with cream and bake in shells. Add fennel and parsley.

MEATS

BEEF, LAMB OR VEAL

Mince fine, add tarragon and parsley, stock to moisten. Heat, but do not boil, and serve on thin slices of toast or rice. Mushrooms may be added.

CHICKEN MINCED WITH MUSHROOMS

Cut chicken up fine and add to pan in which mushrooms have been cooked in butter with a little onion, tarragon, and paprika. Dredge with flour. Add Madeira. Serve in a ring of rice or noodles.

CHICKEN SOUP

Heat chicken with broth. Reduce to pulp in Waring mixer, add milk, and cook in double boiler. Thicken slightly.

CHICKEN POT PIE

Put cut-up cooked chicken in casserole, add a little onion and potato, and moisten with cream sauce. Cover with pastry. Add tarragon if desired.

CHICKEN PILAF

Add minced chicken to rice which has been cooked raw in butter with stock added. A little tomato may be added.

CHICKEN HASHED WITH EGG

Hash chicken, moisten with stock, and serve on toast with poached egg.

DUCK SALMI

Mince left-over duck, add a little onion, mushrooms, and cut-up olives. Heat in stock.

TURKEY

Slice and reheat in gravy with dressing.

TURKEY MINCED

Mince turkey, add onion, and heat with stock. Serve on toast.

TURKEY TIMBALES

Make cream sauce, add turkey minced fine, mold in timbale shape, roll in bread crumbs, and fry in deep fat.

TURKEY PILAF

Fry cooked rice in butter. Add minced turkey and 2 Tbs. tomato. Add broth and cook until done.

EGGS

OMELET

with left-over chicken and mushrooms.

OMELET

with any kind of vegetables or bits of meat and fine herbs.

SCRAMBLED EGGS

with cheese, mushrooms, or left-over vegetables.　Add tarragon and parsley.

CHAPTER XV

ADDITIONAL RECIPES

LIST OF RECIPES

Avocado Soup
Omelet with Sour Cream
Cheese Snacks

Cherries Rhumba
Black Cherry Jelly

AVOCADO SOUP

1 very ripe avocado
3 or 4 cups of stock
1 Tbs. whipping cream to each cup

1 Tbs. lemon juice
1 Tbs. sherry to each cup

Press avocado through coarse strainer into hot stock. Bring to a boil. Season to taste. Stir in cream and lemon. Add sherry.

OMELET WITH SOUR CREAM

Make 4-egg omelet with fine herbs (see page 88). Before turning, add about 2 Tbs. sour cream and fold.

CHEESE SNACKS

1 cup flour
½ tsp. salt
¼ tsp. mustard

Cayenne
4 oz. butter
4 oz. Old English cheese

Sift flour and seasonings. Cut in butter and cheese till crumbly. Work with hands till thoroughly amalgamated.

Form into roll and chill for 12 hours. Cut in thin slices and bake on cooky sheet for 8 to 10 minutes in a moderately hot oven (375° F.).

CHERRIES RHUMBA

Pour contents of 12-oz. can of pitted black cherries into bowl. Drain off juice and cover with rum. Let stand 12 hours and serve with sour cream.

BLACK CHERRY JELLY

1 cup pitted black cherries	4 Tbs. sugar
1 cup cherry juice	Pinch of salt
1 cup orange juice	1 Tbs. brandy
1 Tbs. lemon juice	1½ Tbs. gelatine, dissolved
¼ cup boiling water	in ¼ cup cold water

Dissolve sugar in boiling water, add salt, pour onto gelatine and stir well. Add orange juice, cherry juice, and cherries. Mix well. Add lemon juice and brandy and pour into mold which has been rinsed in cold water. Chill 24 hours.

GENERAL INDEX